THE LIBRARY OF AMERICAN LIVES AND TIMES™

GEORGE WASHINGTON

Leader of a New Nation

Daniel C. Gedacht

The Rosen Publishing Group's
PowerPlus Books™
New York

In loving memory of my father, Leon Gedacht . . .
not a history major, but he would have
enjoyed this just the same

Published in 2004 by The Rosen Publishing Group, Inc.
29 East 21st Street, New York, NY 10010

First Edition

Editor's Note: All quotations have been reproduced as they appeared in the letters and diaries from which they were borrowed. No correction was made to the inconsistent spelling and grammar that was common at the time.

Library of Congress Cataloging-in-Publication Data

Gedacht, Daniel C.
George Washington : leader of a new nation / Daniel C. Gedacht.
p. cm. — (The library of American lives and times)
Summary: Surveys the life of George Washington, the son of a Virginia tobacco planter who became the first president of the United States.
Includes bibliographical references (p.) and index.
ISBN 0-8239-6622-4
1. Washington, George, 1732–1799—Juvenile literature. 2. Presidents—United States—Biography—Juvenile literature. [1. Washington, George, 1732–1799. 2. Presidents.] I. Title. II. Series.
E312.66 .G37 2004
973.4'1'092—dc21

2002005039

Manufactured in the United States of America

Contents

1. "First in the Hearts of His Countrymen" 5
2. Young Surveyor 13
3. Journey to the Ohio River 19
4. Bravery in Battle 25
5. Taxation Without Representation 34
6. Commander in Chief 40
7. Keeping Spirits High 55
8. The Struggle Continues 63
9. The World Turned Upside Down 67
10. Rebellion Against Law 73
11. "Integrity and Firmness is All I Can Promise" 77
12. President of the United States 82
13. "A Wise, a Good, and a Great Man" 93

Timeline 100
Glossary 102
Additional Resources 105
Bibliography 106
Index 107
About the Author 109
Primary Sources 110

1. "First in the Hearts of His Countrymen"

Even before the United States existed, Americans had adopted George Washington as the father of their country. By 1775, the commander in chief of the Continental army was so popular in the colonies that people named their children for him. In the spring of 1776, the Massachusetts town of Stoughtonham was renamed Washington. Since then, a state has been named for him, and his likeness has been placed on the one-dollar bill. Of course, the capital of the country he helped to create bears his name. It is called Washington, D.C.

Washington has been called "first in war, first in peace and first in the hearts of his countrymen." General Henry Lee read these words in Congress after George Washington died. How did the third son of a Virginian tobacco planter rise to become the leader of an army that defeated the British military, and the first president of a new nation? The story of George Washington begins in Virginia in the

Opposite: Gilbert Stuart's 1785 oil portrait of Washington was a new look at the aging statesman, unique in its detail and style. Stuart painted many portraits of Washington, which were then copied and engraved by other artists, contributing to his national popularity.

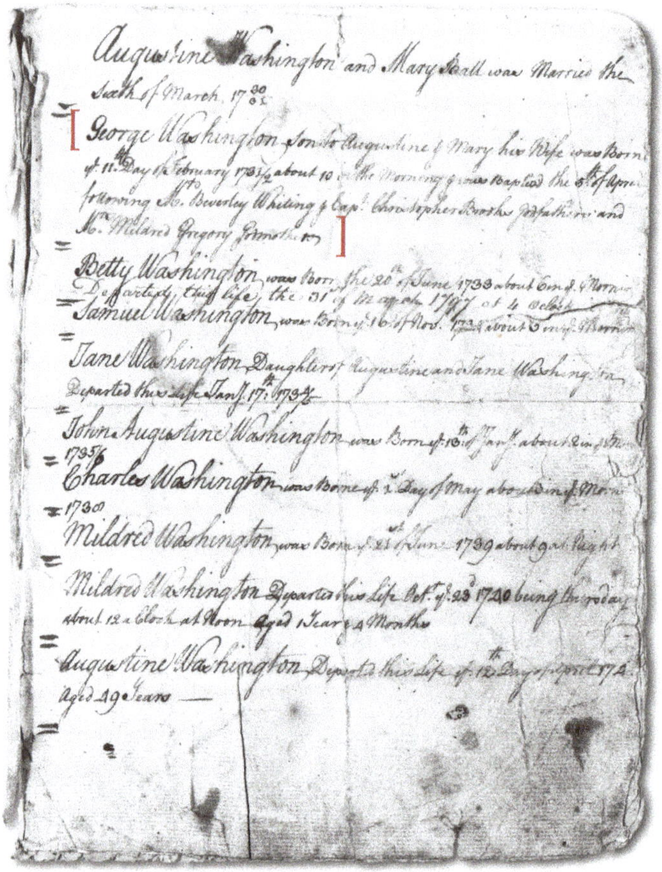
Augustine Washington and Mary Ball was Married the Sixth of March 1730/31

George Washington Son to Augustine & Mary his Wife was Born ye 11th Day of February 1731/2 about 10 in the Morning & was Baptized the 5th of April following Mr. Beverley Whiting & Capt. Christopher Brooks Godfathers and Mrs. Mildred Gregory Godmother

Betty Washington was Born the 20th of June 1733 about 6 in the Morning
Departed this life the 31st of March 1797 at 4 o'clock

Samuel Washington was Born ye 16th of Nov. 1734 about 3 in ye Morning

Jane Washington Daughter of Augustine and Jane Washington Departed this life Jan. 17th 1734/5

John Augustine Washington was Born ye 13th of Jan. about 2 in ye Morning 1735/6

Charles Washington was Born ye 2 Day of May about [illegible] in ye Morning 1738

Mildred Washington was Born ye 21st of June 1739 about 9 at Night

Mildred Washington Departed this Life Oct. ye 23d 1740 being Thursday about 12 a Clock at Noon Aged 1 Year & 4 Months

Augustine Washington Departed this life ye 12th Day of April 1743 Aged 49 Years

As did many eighteenth-century families, the Washingtons recorded important events on the front and back pages of the family Bible. Mention of George Washington's birth is indicated in red brackets.

early 1700s.

Augustine Washington and his wife, Mary Ball Washington, welcomed a new son into the world on February 22, 1732. The family lived at Wakefield Farm, located in Westmoreland County in the British colony of Virginia in North America. They named their son George. George was Mary Ball Washington's first child and Augustine's fifth child. Augustine had been married once before, to Jane Butler. Jane had died in 1729, at thirty years of age. Augustine and Jane had had four children together. Butler, the firstborn, died when he was just a baby. Jane, the youngest, died when she was twelve. Their two other children, Lawrence and Augustine, survived and were George's older

Around 1860, Currier & Ives published this lithograph of Wakefield Farm, George Washington's birthplace. The artist imagined the simple, clapboard cottage pictured here. The Washingtons' actual two-story, brick manor burned down in 1779, and was never rebuilt.

half brothers. Lawrence was fourteen years older than George, and Augustine was twelve years older. After George was born, Augustine and Mary Ball Washington had five more children: Elizabeth, Samuel, John Augustine, Charles, and Mildred. Mildred died when she was a baby.

George's father, Augustine, owned several large tobacco plantations, totaling more than 10,000 acres (4,047 ha). He was a sharp businessman and grew wealthy from farming and from interests in the local iron ore furnaces. He owned many slaves who worked on his land. He grew tobacco and sent it to England, where it was traded for money and goods, such as glass and silver, which were not easily available in the colonies.

When George was a child, his father and mother moved their family from one of their three Virginian plantations to another, finally settling at Ferry Farm on the Rappahannock River. George studied for only a few years in a one-room schoolhouse near Ferry Farm, but he took his education very seriously. Spelling and handwriting were important subjects for children in the eighteenth century, and students practiced by writing in a copybook. George and other children copied the text from such books as *Youths Behaviour, or Decency in Conversation Amongst Men*. These lessons not only helped them to practice handwriting, but also taught young boys the correct behavior for gentlemen in the eighteenth century. In his copybook, George wrote 110 "Rules of Civility and Decent Behavior in Company and Conversation," including:

> *1st Every Action done in Company, ought to be with Some Sign of Respect, to those that are Present.*
>
> . . .
>
> *3rd Shew Nothing to your Friend that may affright him.*
>
> *4th In the Presence of Others Sing not to yourself with a humming Noise, nor Drum with your Fingers or Feet.*

George also admired and studied the manners of his eldest brother, Lawrence. Lawrence had studied in England and had returned to Virginia as an elegant gentleman when George was only six years old. After Lawrence returned from his studies in England, he served in the British colonial forces. He also served as a captain under British admiral Edward Vernon in the failed attack against Spain in Cartagena, Colombia, in 1740–1741, and may have contracted tuberculosis during the expedition. When Lawrence returned from this expedition, Augustine rewarded his oldest son with a gift of land, on which Lawrence built a home he named Mount Vernon. He named the estate for his former commander, Admiral Vernon. In 1743, Lawrence married Anne Fairfax, the daughter of Colonel William Fairfax, who was the cousin and agent of Lord Fairfax. Lord Fairfax was a wealthy Englishman who controlled more than 5 million acres (2 million ha) of land in Virginia.

A portrait of Lawrence shows George's half brother as he looked on his return from England. Lawrence and Augustine received extensive formal schooling, but George did not.

Through Lawrence's marriage, the Washingtons were connected to this powerful family. Lawrence's influence in Virginia grew, and he soon became an adjutant in the militia and a member of the House of Burgesses. The House of Burgesses was established in 1619, soon after the first English settlement was founded in Virginia, and it was the first popularly elected legislature in colonial America.

In 1743, when George was only eleven, his father died and left most of the family's property to Lawrence. George inherited the land and house at Ferry Farm on the Rappahannock River, but the estate was managed by his mother until young George came of age. George spent much of his time at his brother Augustine's home at Wakefield Farm. He sometimes went for long visits to see Lawrence at Mount Vernon, on the Potomac River.

In addition to his Virginian farms, George's father had owned large pieces of land west of the Allegheny Mountains, and this property became Lawrence's when Augustine died. The property was mostly undeveloped forest inhabited by French fur trappers and by Indians who had lived on the land for generations. The Washington family had been granted the land by the king of Britain, but these grants were not recognized by either French settlers or Indian nations. Lawrence Washington and many other wealthy Virginians believed that Virginia should send people to settle the land west of the Alleghenies before the French established towns there and claimed the land for themselves.

George had never been beyond the lands where his family lived. The young man wanted to travel and find adventure. He begged Lawrence to send him on a trip to survey, or to make maps and charts, of Lawrence's frontier land. In 1747, when he was fifteen, George moved to Mount Vernon. He lived there year-round and began his study of surveying and military tactics under the instruction of his brother and other teachers.

At his home, Mount Vernon, Lawrence introduced George Washington to important Virginian statesmen and to the manners of a Virginian gentleman and farmer. Lawrence carefully taught

Although George Washington wrote daily letters to friends and jotted in a journal almost every day of his adult life, some of his most important personal papers no longer exist. When Washington died, his wife, Martha, reportedly burned all their letters. Some family members either gave his letters away or threw them out. Historians also destroyed much of his work, and one scholar even cut Washington's letters into pieces to give to friends. Most of the letters that survive today are kept at the Library of Congress in Washington, D.C., at the University of Virginia, and at Mount Vernon, Washington's home.

his younger half brother how to be a surveyor, a soldier, and a politician. Under Lawrence's instruction and influence, George Washington was becoming an accomplished young man.

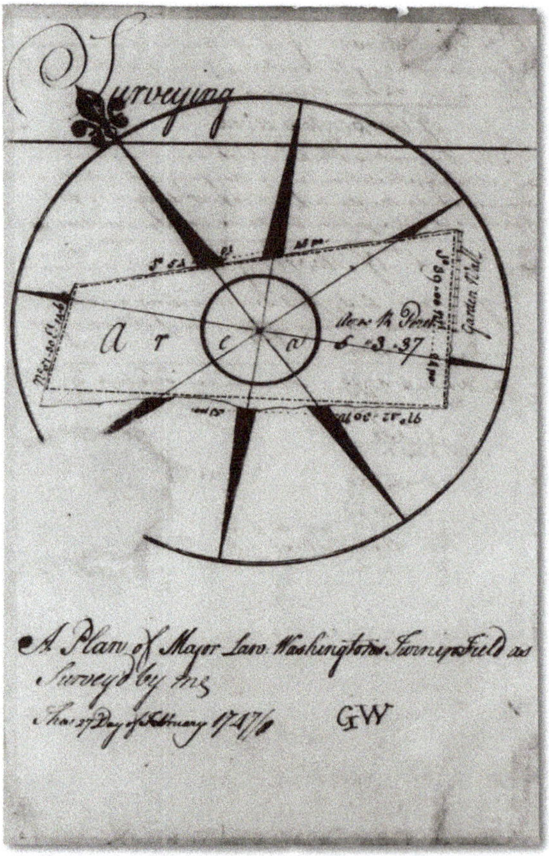

Fifteen-year-old George undertook this survey of Lawrence's Mount Vernon turnip field on February 27, 1747. It is one of 218 pages of lessons and copy work that survive and that chronicle the future statesman's early education.

2. Young Surveyor

While living at Mount Vernon with Lawrence, George Washington became very close with the Fairfax family, especially with young George William Fairfax, who was seven years his senior. George Washington spent much time at the Fairfaxes' home, Belvoir, riding horses, hunting foxes, and continuing his study of surveying. Surveying was an important profession in colonial America. Settlement was pushing steadily west from the Atlantic coast. As settlers arrived in western Virginia, the colony needed people who could survey the land. Surveyors charted land, made maps, and determined the exact boundary lines of property.

Early in 1748, Lord Fairfax announced that he was sending a party to map his lands in the Shenandoah Valley, beyond the Blue Ridge Mountains. After observing George at his surveying studies, Lord Fairfax decided to include him in the expedition. James Genn, the chief surveyor for Prince William County, led the trip, and George's best friend, George William Fairfax, was also in the group. Best of all, George would be paid for his work.

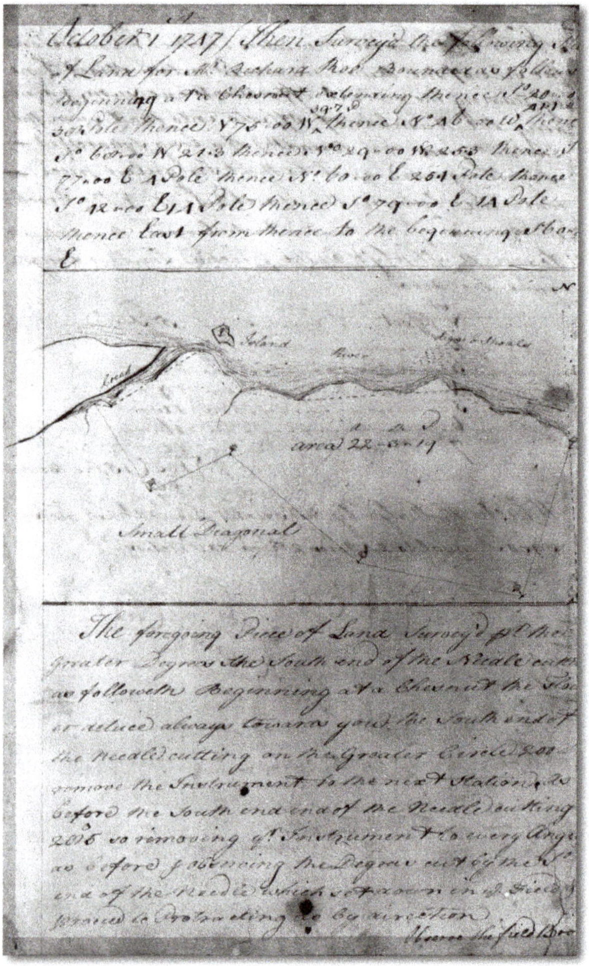

George Washington kept a practical account of his experiences throughout his life. This diary excerpt, dated October 1, 1747, using the Old Style or Julian calendar, is an account of George's early surveys of Virginia and the Shenandoah Valley.

On March 11, 1748, when he was only sixteen years old, George left home for the Shenandoah Valley, prepared to encounter the colonial frontier for the first time. George was shocked at the miserable conditions endured by the Irish, Scottish, and German settlers of western Virginia. The evening that the weary travelers reached the Shenandoah Valley, they spent the night in a log house in the middle of a small clearing. All the men slept together on the floor in one room. Because it was George's first trip, they offered the young man the only bed. According to George's diary, the bedding was filled with lice and fleas. After only a few moments in bed, he put on his clothes and laid on the clean floor with the rest of the men. In addition to meeting European settlers on this trip, George saw Indians for what might have been the first time. During the surveyors' visit with the Indians, the Indians performed a war dance. In the wilderness, young George Washington watched in amazement as the Indian warriors danced around a large fire to the beat of a drum.

Colonial landowners and speculators depended on their surveying tools. This field compass belonged to George Washington and may have been used during his surveys of Lord Fairfax's lands in Virginia.

By the end of the trip, George was an experienced woodsman. He had slept in haystacks, bathed in creeks, and hunted wild turkeys. He had even learned how to cook over a campfire. Lord Fairfax liked George a great deal, and he asked George to help map the boundaries, details, and streets of the new town of Alexandria, Virginia. Thanks to Lord Fairfax, George received another important job in July 1749, when he was appointed official surveyor of Culpeper County, Virginia. Though George was more comfortable sleeping in a bed than on the cold ground around a campfire, he returned to the woods as a surveyor many times during the next years, eager to make his fortune by charting, buying, and selling land. He also began surveying for the Ohio Company, which had been created by Lawrence Washington, Thomas Lee, and several other business partners. In February 1749, the king of Britain had granted the Ohio Company 200,000 acres (80,937 ha) of land along the Ohio River with the possibility of an additional 300,000 acres (121,406 ha) to be allotted later. The original land grant included parts of modern-day West Virginia, Ohio, and Pennsylvania. The company planned to divide the land into plots and then sell it to English farmers. A company trading post at the junction of the Allegheny and Monongahela Rivers would be financially beneficial and would ensure a friendship with the local Indians. Whether he would describe himself as such or not, George had joined his half brother and other wealthy Virginians as a land speculator. In October 1750, George bought land on Bullskin Creek, a tributary of the Shenandoah River, totaling more than 1,400 acres (566.5 ha).

The Ohio Company promised financial success for Lawrence, but he would not be able to enjoy it. By fall 1751, Lawrence had become very ill. He had never fully recovered from his time in Cartagena. His doctor persuaded him to go to Barbados, an island in the Caribbean Sea, hoping that the warm weather would cure him. Lawrence asked George to go with him. After five weeks at sea, they landed on the tropical island. As George wrote in his journal, the brothers were amazed by

George Washington completed this map of the Ohio River valley in 1753. Throughout the seventeenth and eighteenth centuries, the area shown was in dispute between French Canadian traders, Native American nations, and British settlers, as colonial land speculators, including the Washingtons, pushed the frontier farther west.

the "beautiful prospects which on every side presented to our view the fields of Cain, Corn, Fruit Trees, etc. in a delightful Green."

Two weeks after the brothers' arrival, George got smallpox, a terrible disease that killed thousands of people during the eighteenth century. George endured a severe fever and a rash that developed into bumps on his forehead and scalp. After ten days of headache, fever, and body aches, George began to improve, and he soon regained his health. George bore deep scars on his face and body for the rest of his life, but he also developed an immunity to the disease, which would serve him well on the frontier and in military camps. George returned to Virginia to renew the Washingtons' interests in land grants, while Lawrence traveled on to Bermuda, another tropical island. Lawrence soon returned to Virginia, with his health in even greater danger. He arranged his business affairs and died in July 1752. In his will, Lawrence left Mount Vernon to his wife, Anne. The will stated that when Anne died Mount Vernon would be given to their daughter, Sarah, and, in the event of her death, to George. Sarah died shortly after her father, and Lawrence's widow soon remarried. No longer interested in Mount Vernon, she first rented it to George and then sold her life interest in the land to him.

3. Journey to the Ohio River

During his short life, Lawrence Washington had enjoyed influence and friendship with many powerful Virginians. These connections were passed on to George Washington when Lawrence died. George Washington became one of the militia's four district adjutants, the men in charge of overseeing the operations of the force, and earned the rank of major. He also took Lawrence's place as a partner in the powerful Ohio Company. The new governor of Virginia, Robert Dinwiddie, was also a partner and urged the other partners to be strong in claiming the land for themselves on behalf of Britain. The French, however, who had been living and working

C. Dixon is thought to have painted this miniature portrait of Robert Dinwiddie around 1750. Responsible for protecting British interests in the colonies, Dinwiddie led the Virginia militia into war.

In 1749, as French troops led by Captain Céleron de Blainville advanced south through the Ohio Valley along six major rivers, they buried lead plates, such as the one shown here, to mark their conquered territory.

in the Ohio River valley for one hundred years, saw the British as intruders. They worried that the British would make permanent settlements in the wilderness and trade goods with the Indians living in the area, weakening France's hold on the frontier economy. In the summer of 1753, French soldiers and a group of their Indian allies marched south from Lake Erie, killing British settlers and surveyors as they claimed the land for France.

Governor Dinwiddie was sure that Britain would have to fight France to keep the land, and he decided to offer a warning to the French commander stationed at Fort Le Boeuf, near modern-day Waterford, Pennsylvania.

This map, engraved by Thomas Jefferys in 1768, illustrates the relative locations of the French forts throughout the Ohio River valley. Forts Le Boeuf and Presque Isle were constructed just south of Lake Erie.

In the eighteenth century, it was considered unfair to fight without first giving a warning. The problem was how to deliver the message. The land was mountainous and swampy, there were many rivers and streams, and there were no good maps of the territory. Young George Washington volunteered to go to Fort Le Boeuf to deliver the message to Captain Jacques Le Gardeur, sieur de Sainte-Pierre. The governor agreed that the more than 6-foot-tall (2-m-tall) Major Washington, known for his athleticism and knowledge of the frontier, was an excellent choice for the mission. It was Washington's opportunity to make a name for himself and to test his bravery as a man in the wilderness. As he wrote in his journal, "I was commissioned and appointed by the Honorable Robert Dinwiddie to deliver a letter to the Commandant of the French forces on the Ohio [River], and set out on the journey on the same day." The letter in his pocket told the French that the British were very concerned "to know that French forces were erecting forts and making settlements" in what Dinwiddie called British territory. The governor of Virginia ordered the French to leave immediately.

The trip into the valley was a difficult one for Washington and his party, which was made up of interpreters and guides. Winter had come early. The weather changed from heavy rain to heavy snow, and soon the streams were swollen. At Logstown, a French trading post deep in the wilderness, Washington met a Seneca

Indian chief named Half King. Half King provided guides and advice for Washington on the best route to Fort Le Boeuf.

On the trip, Washington passed by several French forts that were protected by armed men. He traveled through a thick wilderness that hid hostile Indians, French soldiers, and French fur trappers. Washington gathered information about the battle that was brewing in the Ohio River valley from soldiers who had abandoned the French army, friendly Indians, and prominent French officers. After one month, Washington reached the French commandant at Fort Le Boeuf and delivered the message to him. While he waited for the commander's reply, Washington inspected the fort and found evidence, in the form of several hundred new canoes, of France's plans to seize control of the Ohio River and all of its tributaries. Soon after, he began his return journey, carrying Captain La Gardeur's reply to Governor Dinwiddie. The journey home was even more difficult than the trip there. It continued to rain and snow, and when the streams froze, there was little fresh water to drink. The horses were exhausted, and the men had to walk much of the way. On one occasion, after working all day to build a raft with which to cross the Allegheny River, Washington fell off the raft when it hit a big chunk of ice. He plunged into the deep, icy water and nearly died.

Finally, on January 16, 1754, two and a half months after his journey began, Washington reported the French

In a painting attributed to Daniel Huntington, Washington *(left)* and his companion Christopher Gist cross the icy Allegheny River on a small raft. The painting was first exhibited in 1843. It inspired an engraving that was widely published throughout the mid-nineteenth century to illustrate book and magazine accounts of Washington's adventure.

commandant's answer to Governor Dinwiddie. The French soldiers would not leave. Soon news of his trip to the Ohio River, including excerpts from Washington's journal and the threatening response from the French commandant, was in every newspaper in Virginia. Washington's journal was published in its entirety in both Virginia and England. The colony prepared to fight. Washington was promoted to lieutenant colonel for his brave work, and he was made second in command under Colonel Joshua Fry.

4. Bravery in Battle

The first full-scale battle of the French and Indian War took place in 1754. Lieutenant Colonel George Washington led a group of Virginia militiamen to defend British territory in what is now Pennsylvania. They headed toward the junction of the Allegheny and Monongahela Rivers, the "forks of the Ohio," where British soldiers had been building a fort. About 50 miles (80 km) from their destination, British scouts told Washington that on April 17, French soldiers had captured the nearly completed fort and named it Fort Duquesne. During the following months, Washington worked tirelessly to mend diplomatic relations with Indian chiefs, engaged in mild skirmishes with French forces, and planned for a full-scale attack. When Washington's commanding officer was thrown from his horse and killed, Washington was promoted to colonel and was put in charge of the entire expedition. Anxious about the coming conflict, Washington ordered his men, numbering only 284, to construct a simple, defensive stockade at a place called Great Meadows, 50 miles (80 km) southwest of Fort Duquesne. Washington called it

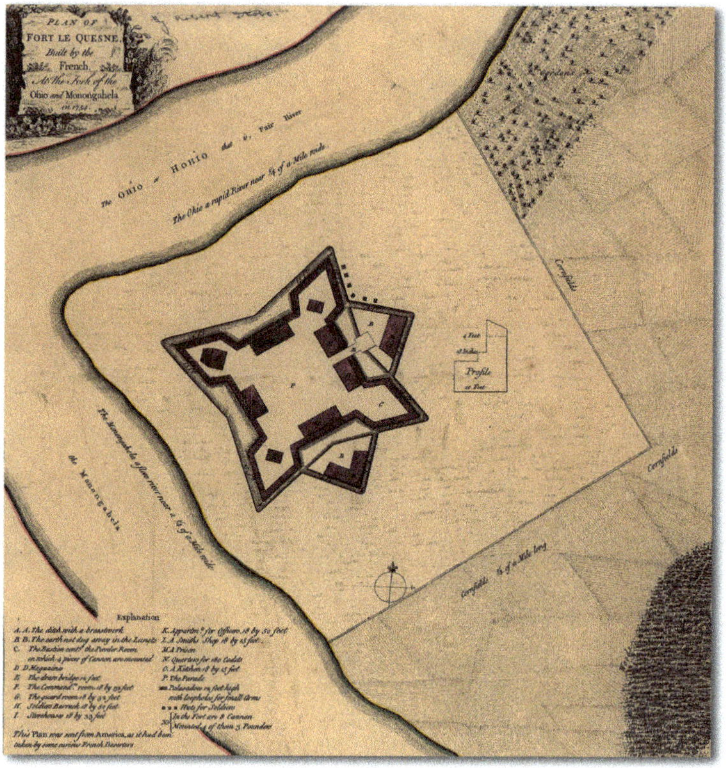

Thomas Jefferys's 1768 engraved map of Fort Duquesne, also known as Fort Le Quesne, shows the French stockade as it appeared in 1754. When Washington approached the fort that year, the French forces stationed there numbered 1,000 men and were guarded by 18 cannons.

Fort Necessity, because the fort was built on low, soggy land that offered few natural advantages.

At the end of May, a small group of French soldiers approached Washington's fort to gather information about the British troops stationed there. The group quietly retreated to relay information to their French commanders. The French returned in larger numbers and attacked on July 3. Plagued by strong rains and a poor defensive position, Washington was forced to surrender Fort Necessity by midnight that night. He and his men were allowed to leave the following day.

Washington returned home depressed by defeat, illness, and the criticisms of some colonials who believed that he had mismanaged his forces. Nevertheless, he immediately began recruiting new soldiers with whom to attack the French. At the same time, Governor Dinwiddie demoted all Virginian officers and made them less powerful than officers from Britain. This meant that Washington, demoted from colonel to captain, would have to take orders from the British officers he had once commanded. Washington was insulted, and he resigned from the militia. Though angry about his demotion, Washington wrote to a friend, "I shall have the consolation of knowing, that I have opened the way" for Britain's eventual victory over the French.

The war between France and Britain did not end when Washington left the militia, and in the early spring of 1755, another opportunity arose for him to serve. He was appointed a volunteer aide-de-camp to British general Edward Braddock, and he marched with Braddock and the British regular army against the French soldiers at Fort Duquesne. In boasting about his new position to his younger brother John, Washington wrote that he only took orders from General Braddock and could "give orders to all which must be implicitly obeyed." Braddock's mission was a bloody failure, however. On July 9, the British and colonial troops, numbering more than 1,400, were defeated at the Battle of the Monongahela River by a combined force of fewer than nine hundred French, Canadian, and Indian men. The fighting was fierce, and General Braddock was killed in battle. Washington was not wounded, but, as he wrote to his mother, "I had four bullets through my Coat, and two Horses shot [out from] under me." Another bullet went through his hat but left Washington unharmed. Despite a recent bout with a severe illness, which at times had left him delirious and bent over in pain, Washington successfully led the British retreat through heavy fire, saving what remained of the army. Though the mission was the subject of debate and

Captain Washington, on horseback and wearing the dark blue uniform of the Virginia militia, leads his men in the Battle of the Monongahela River. Junius Brutus Stearns painted this scene in oil around 1851.

criticism in the months that followed, Washington was called a hero. He was appointed colonel in the Virginia militia and was responsible for defending the 350-mile-long (563-km-long) western frontier.

The colonial assembly and Governor Dinwiddie had commissioned Washington and his troops to defend Virginia through 1758, but the colonial government did not provide the men with much assistance. Washington struggled to recruit soldiers, to organize the purchase of provisions, and to maintain order at the forts. Soldiers stationed at frontier forts found life difficult. The wooden barracks were cold in the winter, hot in the summer, and leaky when it rained. The soldiers suffered from overwork, exhaustion, boredom, and disease. Smallpox killed men at several forts. The lack of fresh fruits and vegetables left soldiers vulnerable to scurvy, and unclean cooking conditions led to the spread of dysentery. The British soldiers feared that French and Indian forces lurked behind every tree and patrolled every road. Frontier settlers fled their small towns and isolated farms for the safety of the Atlantic coast.

After three years of leading minor skirmishes and unsuccessful attempts to defeat France, Washington was put in command of seven hundred men from four colonies. This British force finally captured Fort Duquesne in November 1758. With only days left before his troops were scheduled to disband for the winter, Washington and his fellow officers led the British and colonial forces toward

the fort. From a distance of more than 10 miles (16 km), they saw smoke billowing up from the site. When they reached the junction of the Allegheny and Monongahela Rivers, all that remained of the fort were its smoldering ashes. The French had burned the fort and fled. Though perhaps disappointed that their bravery had not been tested in battle, the British and colonial forces celebrated their victory. They rebuilt Fort Duquesne and named the new garrison Fort Pitt for Secretary of State William Pitt.

Following this success, Washington again resigned from the militia. The French and Indian War continued without him, finally ending in 1763. Britain won, and France gave up their strategic military forts.

As the war came to an end, Washington settled down to start his own family and establish himself as a community leader, businessman, and farmer. On January 6, 1759, he married Martha Dandridge Custis, a wealthy widow. Martha had two young children, Jacky and Patsy. Washington adored the children and treated them as if they were his own. Martha and he never had children together. After having been elected as a representative to the House of Burgesses in the summer of 1758, Washington began his political career when the house convened on February 22. During the following decade, Washington spent most of his time farming and

---

Opposite: In 1772, Charles Willson Peale painted the only likeness of Washington made before the American Revolution. He wears a gorget, a crescent-shaped piece of metal that represents the suits of armor worn by medieval knights. Under his left arm, he carries a fowler, or hunting rifle, which identifies Washington as a man of the American frontier.

Washington was determined to reform the one-crop system that most Virginian farmers used, calling the old-fashioned way of farming tobacco "ruinous, unprofitable and destructive" to the land. Washington was not the first farmer to use a plan of crop rotation, but he was one of the earliest to make long-term plans using several crops. He hoped that this system would keep the soil strong for years. His system was simple. A field would be planted with wheat one year, buckwheat the next, wheat again the following year, and grass and clover the fourth year. During the fifth year, Washington would plant potatoes or corn in the field. He would leave certain plants, such as buckwheat and clover, unharvested, allowing them to rot in the ground and become fertilizer. This method let the soil rest and recover nutrients and provided grazing land for cattle while the ground lay fallow. Washington also tried new farming techniques that were called new husbandry. One of these techniques was deep plowing. Generally, farmers plowed only the top few inches of soil, but Washington plowed between 8 and 10 inches (20–25 cm) deep to mix the soil better. Washington also used fertilizers to improve the soil's texture, and he planted his seeds in regularly spaced rows to make weeding more efficient.

expanding the lands of Mount Vernon.

Times were happy for the most part, but the Washingtons also had their share of sadness. Washington noted in his journal on June 19, 1773, that at "about five o'clock poor Patsy Custis died suddenly." Washington's stepdaughter was seventeen years old and had long suffered from epilepsy. George Washington wrote to a friend that he hoped "the sweet innocent girl" had gone to "a more happy, & peaceful abode."

This 1757 painting by John Wollaston of Martha Dandridge Custis, George Washington's future wife, was begun just before the death of Martha's first husband, Daniel Parke Custis. The young Martha Custis was already an experienced mother and homemaker.

5. Taxation Without Representation

While George Washington lived at Mount Vernon and tended to his plantation, trouble was brewing in Boston, Massachusetts. The French and Indian War had been expensive, and the British government had many debts to pay. Great Britain made money from the colonies by imposing taxes. The colonies did not have representatives in Parliament, and many colonists believed that it was unfair for Parliament to impose additional taxes on them if colonists did not have a voice in the government. Many colonists grew unhappy with Parliament, and some blamed Britain's king, George III. A few colonists even began to think about independence. One of the first major conflicts of what would become the colonial struggle for independence happened in Boston on March 5, 1770. A group of fifty or sixty angry colonists gathered before a small group of British soldiers in front of a customhouse. The colonial mob began taunting the armed men, throwing rocks, pieces of coal, and oyster shells at the soldiers. A British soldier fired his weapon, inciting a riot. When the angry mob cleared, five Bostonians, including a black sailor and former slave named Crispus Attucks, were dead. Revolutionaries, including Samuel Adams, named the event the Boston Massacre and used it to raise support for their protests against the British government.

George III, king of Great Britain, appears in silk and fur coronation robes in Allan Ramsay's oil painting, made between 1761 and 1762. The nearly life-size painting hung in the Governor's Palace in Williamsburg, Virginia.

The situation worsened on the night of December 16, 1773. A group of Boston colonists disguised as Indians snuck onto cargo ships and dumped 342 chests of tea into Boston Harbor to protest the tax on tea. This event was called the Boston Tea Party. In response, Great Britain passed the Coercive Acts, known by Americans as the Intolerable Acts, in an attempt to bring the colonies back under the control of King George III. These acts gave Great Britain direct power over North American colonial affairs.

The colonists' rebellion in Massachusetts quickly

Five separate laws comprised what the colonists came to know collectively as the Intolerable Acts. The Quartering Act required colonial citizens to house and feed British soldiers. The Boston Port Bill closed the port of Boston to all colonists until the damages from the Boston Tea Party were paid. The Administration of Justice Act stated that a British official charged with a crime would be sent back to England for trial. This law meant that colonists could do nothing to punish soldiers or officials of the British government. The Massachusetts Government Act removed the Massachusetts colonial government from power and gave the British royal governor complete control. Finally, the Quebec Act gave control of the land between the Ohio and Mississippi Rivers to the British governor of Quebec.

spread to other colonies. In May 1774, the royal governor of Virginia, John Murray, earl of Dunmore, dissolved the House of Burgesses, ending more than 160 years of representative government in Virginia. Burgess Thomas Jefferson wrote that "we must boldly take . . . a stand." Washington and the other burgesses soon met at the Raleigh Tavern in Williamsburg, Virginia, to address the Intolerable Acts and the dissolution of the House of Burgesses. In July 1774, Washington, along with other burgesses and leading residents of the district, wrote the Fairfax County Resolves. This document asked the colonists to support Boston and to stop importing or buying British goods. The resolves also called for the estab-

Through the spring and the summer of 1774, the former members of the House of Burgesses met at Raleigh Tavern in Williamsburg, Virginia. There George Washington and Virginian statesman George Mason drafted a revolutionary statement of the colony's fundamental rights, which came to be known as the Fairfax County Resolves.

lishment of a continental congress to decide how to proceed. The Fairfax Resolves were made public on July 18 and were greeted with much support. On September 5, 1774, representatives from twelve of the thirteen colonies met in Philadelphia for the First Continental Congress. George Washington attended as a representative from Virginia.

Many representatives, including Washington, hoped to resolve the colonies' differences with Britain peacefully. While in Philadelphia, Washington wrote to a friend "that it is the ardent wish of the warmest advocates for liberty, that peace and tranquility, upon constitutional grounds, may be restored" and that war may be avoided. Washington did, however, support the actions of Boston's patriots in fighting unjust laws. "None of them will ever submit to the loss of those valuable rights & privileges . . . [of] Life, Liberty, & property," he wrote.

By April 1775, colonial militiamen in Concord, Massachusetts, had begun stockpiling weapons. British general and governor of Massachusetts Thomas Gage ordered that the rebels' weapons be seized. Gage assembled a group of soldiers to march to Concord at midnight on April 18. The revolutionaries had planned for

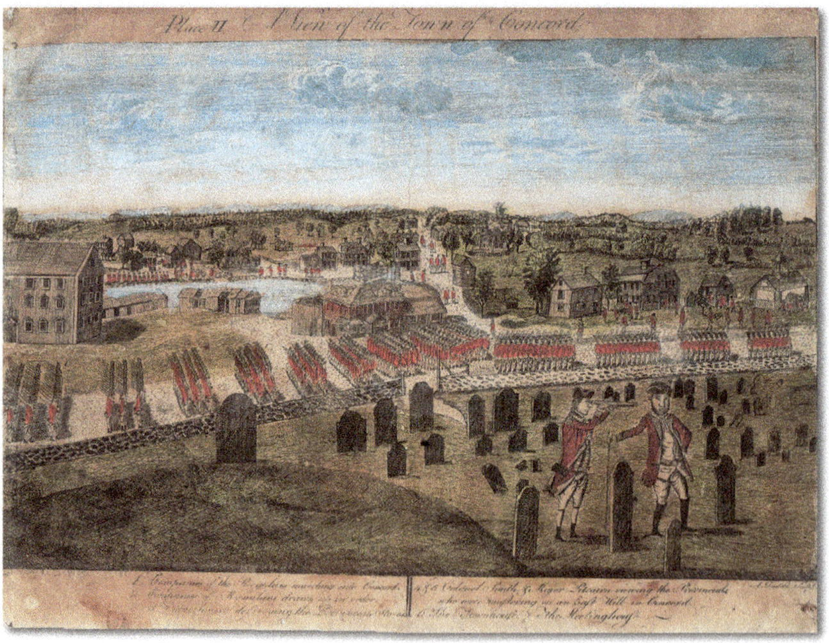

British regulars, as soldiers of the king of Britain were commonly called, can be seen marching through the streets of Concord, Massachusetts, in this 1775 engraving by Sidney L. Smith, based on a painting by Amos Doolittle. The original painting was based on eyewitness accounts.

this response. The chairman of the colonial Committee of Safety sent Paul Revere and William Dawes to ride from Boston to Lexington, by separate routes, to warn patriots Samuel Adams and John Hancock that the British soldiers intended to arrest them. Revere and Dawes stopped at houses along the way to alert people of the news. After delivering the message to Adams and Hancock, Revere and Dawes met up and continued on the road to Concord, where the revolutionaries' weapons and supplies were stored. A third rider, Samuel Prescott, met them along the way, and the three men continued to warn people until they were caught by a British patrol unit. Prescott escaped and conveyed the news to the patriots at Concord. This advance warning gave the Lexington militia time to organize before the British arrived.

At dawn on April 19, British major John Pitcairn and Lieutenant Colonel Francis Smith led the British soldiers into Lexington, where they met the Colonial militia commanded by Captain John Parker. No one knows who fired the first shot, but a volley of gunfire broke out and killed eight colonists. The militia retreated, and the British soldiers continued to march to Concord. After the British set fire to the armory, the colonists responded, routing the British regulars at Concord's North Bridge. The British retreated into Boston and occupied the city under siege for eleven months.

6. Commander in Chief

On May 10, 1775, the Second Continental Congress met in Philadelphia. Again, George Washington attended as a delegate from Virginia and joined the delegates in laying out a plan for the future. During the coming months, the colonists would prepare for war even as they tried to maintain peace with Britain. The patriots began military preparations, but they also sent a document known as the Olive Branch Petition to George III. The petition requested that the king revoke the Intolerable Acts. Parliament and the king denied this request.

On June 15, 1775, George Washington was appointed commander in chief of the as-yet-unformed Continental forces. Washington refused the salary offered by Congress, instead asking only that Congress pay his expenses at the end of the war. Two days after Washington's appointment took place in Philadelphia, the Boston militia, which had retreated to a town near Boston after the fighting at Lexington and Concord, secretly set up camp on Breed's Hill, overlooking the city of Boston. Overnight the militia prepared their defenses.

British general Sir William Howe led two unsuccessful charges against the Colonial encampment. On the third try, he was successful, but the battle was not an easy victory for the British. Of the 2,400 British soldiers present, more than 1,000 were hurt. Approximately 440 Colonial soldiers were wounded. Although the battle, today commonly called the Battle of Bunker Hill, was a defeat for the colonists, their strength proved that they had a chance against the British. The battle also taught the British that they had underestimated the ragged, untrained Colonial army.

Washington journeyed to Cambridge, Massachusetts, at the end of June to take command of his troops.

When Washington arrived in New York on June 25, 1775, details of the colonial defeat at the Battle of Bunker Hill, shown here, awaited him. He soon set off for Boston, where the army lacked soldiers, officers, staff, and supplies.

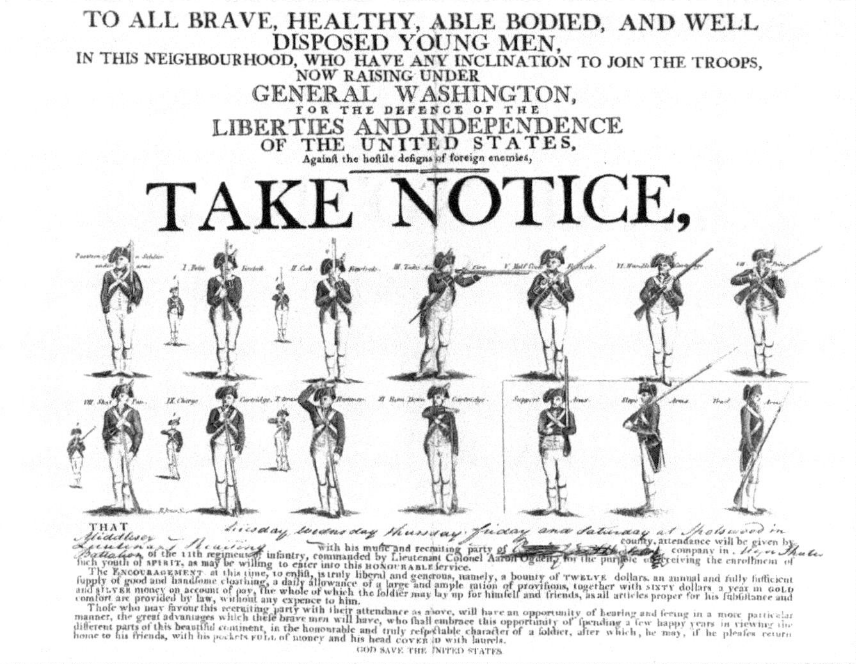

A 1775 broadside calls for "ALL BRAVE, HEALTHY, ABLE BODIED, AND WELL DISPOSED YOUNG MEN" to enlist in General Washington's army "FOR THE DEFENCE OF THE LIBERTIES AND INDEPENDENCE OF THE UNITED STATES, AGAINST THE HOSTILE DESIGNS OF FOREIGN ENEMIES."

Washington strongly believed that the colonies had to fight as a single unit to succeed. Prior to the conflict at Breed's Hill, the revolutionaries had thought of themselves as citizens of individual colonies. In his general orders issued on July 4, 1775, Washington said Continental soldiers were "troops of the United Provinces of North America," and were not simply a Colonial militia.

During this time, Washington wrote several letters to his wife, Martha, in which the inexperienced commander questioned his ability to accomplish the daunting task that had been put before him. Although Martha traveled to be with him in Cambridge in December and would join him at camp each winter during the war, Washington would not see his home at Mount Vernon again until 1781.

On February 16, 1776, Washington held a war council with his top officers. The previous month, news had arrived that George III intended to hire mercenary soldiers to suppress the colonial insurrection. This news was a bold declaration of the Crown's attitude toward its revolutionary subjects. The patriots decided that the Colonial forces needed to act before British reinforcements arrived in the spring. The patriots decided to occupy Dorchester Heights, a peninsula of high ground that overlooked Boston Harbor from the southeast.

The harbor teemed with British warships, and the narrow neck of land connecting Boston with the mainland was heavily fortified with British troops. The revolutionaries had positioned the first mortars at the Heights by March 2. After three days, the British could see a stockade with cannons staring down at them from the Heights, and 2,400 colonial soldiers were encamped on the high ground. When a magnificent storm hit the following day, British commander General Howe decided that the colonial stronghold would be too difficult to attack. Not eager to sacrifice thousands of men to take the fort, Howe sent a message to Washington warning

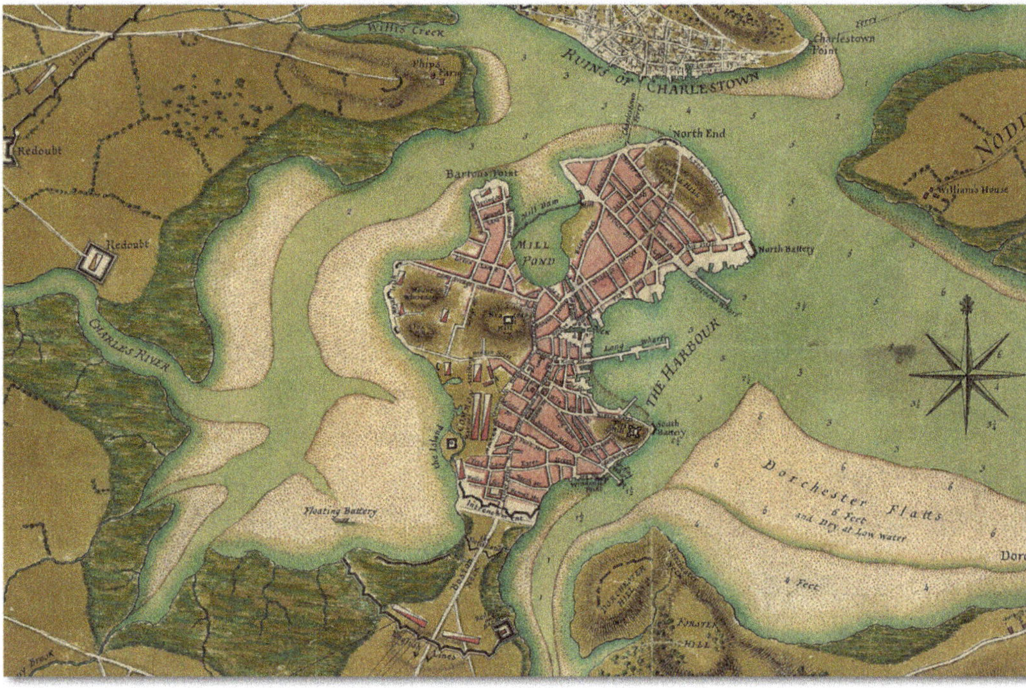

From the hills of Dorchester Heights, Washington's army looked down on the city of Boston and its wide harbor, shown here in a detail from a 1776 map by Sir Thomas Hyde Page. However, even this strategic location would not have protected the inexperienced revolutionary soldiers from the well-trained British forces. It was luck and foul weather that saved the Americans.

him that if the colonists stationed at the Heights fired on the British ships in the harbor below, the British would burn Boston. If Washington did not fire upon the ships, Howe promised that the British would leave. Washington did not fire his cannons, and on March 17, General Howe's men boarded their ships and evacuated Boston as promised. Washington was not yet aware of how good his luck had been. If the rebels had been forced to fight the British in hand-to-hand combat at the Heights, the inexperienced colonial forces would have been destroyed by the well-trained British regulars, and the war for independence might have been over in a matter of hours.

The colonists did not know where the British were headed, but General Washington believed that New York City was Britain's next target. He worried that losing this city "would give [the British] Command of the Country," and he immediately marched his troops to the city. On April 13, Washington arrived in Manhattan with nearly twenty thousand soldiers and issued a warning to the residents about the possibility of a British invasion. The island of Manhattan was ideal for occupation by a naval power such as Britain, but it would be very difficult for Washington's foot soldiers to defend. Under Washington's direction, the Continental army constructed Fort Washington in northern Manhattan and built a line of cannons that overlooked New York's harbor on the Hudson River. Washington spread out his troops over both sides of the East River and all around Manhattan. Patriot ships were intentionally sunk at the mouth of the East River to prevent British ships from passing.

A fleet of 130 British ships arrived in New York's harbor on June 29, 1776. The British forces were made up of British regulars and German mercenaries known as Hessians. The British anchored their ships along the shores of Long Island and Staten Island, out of range of the revolutionaries' cannons, hoping that the reb-

A 1777 map engraved by William Faden tracks the British forces in New York and New Jersey. General Howe's troops were encamped throughout the five modern boroughs of New York City and along the western shore of the Hudson River to the Tappan Sea, today's Tappan Zee.

els would come to their senses, and that the two sides would avoid conflict. Washington and Howe each waited anxiously for the other to make the next move.

While Washington was busy with military matters, the Continental Congress was in Philadelphia debating the status of the colonies. It had been unclear whether the colonies were fighting to be an independent country, or simply to overturn the Intolerable Acts. Some delegates, including Samuel Adams and John Hancock, were in favor of revolution and independence. Other delegates only wanted a more powerful role in Parliament. On June 7, 1776, Richard Henry Lee of Virginia formally proposed that Congress declare the thirteen American colonies independent from Britain. In support of Lee's proposition, Congress appointed a committee to prepare a declaration of the colonists' sovereignty. Thomas Jefferson, John Adams, Benjamin Franklin, Roger Sherman, and Robert Livingston were the chosen committee members.

Thomas Jefferson was given the primary role of drafting the declaration. Jefferson firmly believed that men had natural rights, which included life, liberty, and the pursuit of happiness. He believed that no government could take away these basic human rights. Jefferson prepared a draft of the document by the end of June. After great debate, Lee's proposition was approved on July 2. On July 4, 1776, Congress approved the Declaration of Independence. Now the rebels' mission was clear. America was fighting for its freedom.

On July 3, large numbers of British soldiers landed on Staten Island. Washington tried to keep the colonists' spirits high and to rally support for the fight despite this threat. On July 9, he announced Congress's adoption of the Declaration of Independence and led an American independence celebration in New York.

Vice Admiral R. Howe led the British fleet to New York. He is shown here in an engraving by J. Chapman, who copied the likeness from a painting by John Singleton Copley.

On July 13, General Howe's brother, Vice Admiral Richard Howe, arrived. Some 150 more ships were to follow. Ninety-six British ships dropped anchor in New York's harbor on August 12 and 13. Twenty more ships arrived the following day, further strengthening the British forces. Though Washington and his men enjoyed several minor victories, the patriots grew anxious. The British were closing in.

On August 22, more than eight thousand British soldiers landed at Gravesend Bay, Long Island, a sheltered coastline just south of the Narrows that divided Staten Island and Brooklyn. The patriots, based in Brooklyn Heights under the command of General John Sullivan, had defenses extending south and southwest toward the hills, just north of Flatbush. On August 26, the British forces maneuvered into Brooklyn and attacked the advanced Colonial defenses from behind. The patriots retreated to Brooklyn Heights, fearful of a full-scale British attack. The first full-fledged fight of the war, the Battle of Brooklyn, had been lost by the patriots. While Washington's men waited for a second British attack, the British navy entered Flushing Bay through the Long Island Sound. The Americans were virtually surrounded. By August 29, Washington realized that by dividing his forces across Brooklyn and Manhattan he had left the army extremely vulnerable. He decided to retreat. In the middle of the night, while navigating through heavy fog and rain, Washington's army quietly evacuated Brooklyn, rowing silently across the East River to Manhattan.

There were several more battles around the city during September and October. Washington met Howe's forces at the Battle of Kip's Bay on September 15, 1776. As the Continental forces began to fall, Washington exposed himself to enemy fire by riding in front of the troops to try, in vain, to rally the men. The patriots gave up ground and allowed the British to advance. A colonial victory at the Battle of Harlem Heights on September 16 and a colonial defeat at the Battle of White Plains on October 28 followed. By mid-October, the British had captured Manhattan and the surrounding area. Washington retreated to New Jersey. His bad judgment in splitting his army almost cost him the war at this early stage. Washington's force suffered few casualties, but he was viciously criticized by many of his men and fellow officers. Over the following months, there was little activity, and Washington moved his troops to a camp in northern Pennsylvania.

On the night of December 25, Washington sat in the cold with fewer than five thousand soldiers. Across the Delaware River, there was a small group of British and Hessian soldiers stationed in Trenton, New Jersey. In the dark of night, Washington and his men crossed the icy Delaware River to launch a surprise attack on the British army and their Hessian mercenaries the following day. The unexpected attack began as a fierce snowstorm buffeted the weary patriots. The assault was a success. Within an hour, the Americans had captured nearly one thousand prisoners without suffering a single loss. The victory at Trenton rallied support for Washington. Two days later, Congress gave him the authority to raise troops and supplies from the colonies directly, to arrest soldiers who did not accept Continental money as payment for their service, and to appoint officers. Washington kept his troops on the march, taking advantage of their small numbers and their lack of heavy supplies. On January 3, 1777, he finished the winter campaign in New Jersey by capturing the British fort at Princeton. Then he set up a winter camp in Morristown, New Jersey, and rebuilt the wearied army with new enlistments.

During the summer of 1777, General Howe changed his focus from controlling New York to advancing on Philadelphia. This Pennsylvanian city was the colonial capital and the original seat of Congress. Washington and his men posed little obstacle to the advancing British forces at the Battle of the Brandywine on September 11. Outwitting and outmaneuvering Washington, Howe and his troops marched into Philadelphia on September 26. On October 3, 1777, George Washington planned to take General Howe and his nine thousand troops by surprise at their encampment in the town of Germantown, 5 miles (8 km) northwest of

Early in the Revolution, many blacks fought on the side of the British, because Britain offered their black veterans freedom in return for their military service. Although blacks had been welcomed in the New England militias, Congress had initially decided against enlisting blacks in the Continental army. Congress needed the support of southern states, and most southern plantation owners were against arming slaves with guns. Eventually, in 1777, when the Continental army was desperate for more men, the government allowed black soldiers to enlist. As the war spread to the South, Congress offered to pay South Carolinian slave owners $1,000 for male slaves. The slaves would not be paid, but at the end of the war, those who had served "well and faithfully" would receive their freedom.

Philadelphia. Washington planned to march four different units in separate groups at night, then surround and attack Howe's headquarters at sunrise. The plan, Washington's first offensive strategy in nearly a year, was well advised. At first, victory seemed assured. But heavy fog and smoke covered the scene, and one group of soldiers marched down the wrong road while another accidentally alerted the British to the coming attack. Chaos broke out. The British regulars were approaching from the rear. Two Continental brigades accidentally fired upon each other. The patriots were forced to retreat more than 20 miles (32 km). Despite another embarrassing defeat, Washington did not lose hope. On October 5, 1777, he wrote in his General Orders that "the enemy are not [invincible] against a vigorous attack . . . [our soldiers] will remember and assure themselves that on the next occasion . . . inspired by the cause of freedom in which they are engaged, they will be victorious."

Previous spread: Washington stands at the bow of a small boat crossing the icy Delaware River in Emmanuel Gottlieb Leutze's romanticized painting. The Continental army launched its attack on the British forces at Trenton to put an end to the regulars' advance toward Philadelphia.

7. Keeping Spirits High

On October 17, 1777, Congress received good news. Continental general Horatio Gates had defeated British general John Burgoyne at Saratoga, New York. This battle was the first major victory for the Americans, and to many it proved that the Continental army was a match for the British. On the heels of Gates's victory, patriots Thomas Jefferson, Benjamin Franklin, and Silas Deane persuaded France to sign the Franco-American Treaty of Amity and Commerce on February 6, 1778. France, a great rival of Britain, had been secretly supplying Congress with military supplies and money for the American Revolution since 1776. Until Gates's victory, France had been unwilling to

By defeating the British at Saratoga, General Horatio Gates, shown here in a 1782 portrait by Charles Willson Peale, regained control of the Hudson River valley for the Americans.

On October 8, 1777, after three weeks of fighting, General Burgoyne retreated to the hills of Saratoga. There 20,000 Continental troops surrounded the British and Hessian soldiers and forced them to surrender. John Trumbull illustrated the surrender, when General Gates refused to accept his enemy's sword and instead invited Burgoyne into his tent.

support openly what might have been a losing cause. Gates's victory was a turning point in the war, but it also highlighted Washington's defeats in contrast. In the following months, Gates, Washington's former adviser Thomas Mifflin, and Brigadier General Thomas Conway plotted to force Washington to resign from the army. Instead of achieving its aim, however, this plot, known as the Conway Cabal, only served to strengthen support for Washington and spur the patriot cause.

By December 1777, most of the fighting had ended

for the year. Washington's army, ill-equipped to stage a full-scale attack on Philadelphia or even to defend patriot forts outside of the city, settled down at Valley Forge, Pennsylvania. Martha Washington joined her husband there, and she raised his spirits by entertaining and overseeing his household, seeing to the care of both Washington's fellow officers and the common soldiers.

Despite the support of Martha Washington, the Continental troops at Valley Forge suffered great hardships. The weather was snowy and cold, uniforms and shoes were old and torn, and food was scarce. Smallpox was widespread in the camp, and many men died. Washington's troops were truly war weary. As Washington wrote in a letter to Patrick Henry, " . . . for several days past, we have experienced little less than famine in camp." However, he wrote, "Naked and starving as they are, we cannot enough admire the incomparable patience and fidelity of the soldiery." Congress encouraged Washington to commandeer supplies from local civilians, but Washington refused to undermine the patriot cause by angering the poor citizens.

George Washington recognized that the revolution-

Next spread: In William T. Trego's 1883 painting, George Washington, on horseback, reviews the war-weary Continental army encamped at Valley Forge. Fearing for the lives of his troops and the future of the Revolution, Washington spoke out against Congress, which had failed to provide supplies, and against Pennsylvanians, who had refused to let Washington's troops spend the winter in nearby towns.

Charles Willson Peale is believed to have painted this portrait of Baron Friedrich von Steuben between 1782 and 1784.

Volunteers from Poland, Germany, and France helped in the fight against Britain. Baron Friedrich von Steuben was a Prussian officer who brought discipline to Washington's army. French general Chevalier Louis Lebèque de Presle Duportail served in the Engineering Corps of the army, designing defense plans and helping to construct forts. Polish colonel Thaddeus Kosciusko also supervised the building of fortifications. His countryman, General Casimir Pulaski, was the commander of the Continental Cavalry, an army unit that fought on horseback. A wealthy noble in France, the Marquis de Lafayette arrived in the colonies in 1777, and volunteered to serve under Washington. Lafayette convinced France to provide money and supplies for the American cause, and he even spent much of his own money to help the colonies fight. Some of the foreigners who helped the colonies in the Revolution were drawn to help the patriots because of a romantic desire for glory in battle. Other volunteers supported the colonial quest for freedom, and some men simply wanted to help defeat Britain.

aries needed to be better trained and organized. His men were just local militiamen fighting together. It would take a well-trained, professional army to defeat Britain. Washington convinced Congress to purchase better supplies for the soldiers at Valley Forge. Congress also supported Washington's troops by sending Baron Friedrich von Steuben, a volunteer from Prussia, to Valley Forge. Steuben was an experienced soldier and, as he proved at Valley Forge, a competent drillmaster. Washington made him a major general and asked him to retrain the ragtag

A 1778 French map follows the American and British armies during the Battle of Monmouth. Under the command of Charles Lee, the Continental army was forced to withdraw. Then Washington appeared, rallied the troops, and forced the British to retreat to safety under the cover of night.

Continental army. Soon, the Continental army was marching and fighting like a professional army. Their strength, courage, and skill were tested at the victorious Battle of Monmouth on June 28, 1778. Sir Henry Clinton, General Howe's second in command, saw for the first time the power of the united American army and a preview of the battles that lay ahead.

8. The Struggle Continues

During much of 1779, the British and Continental forces experienced minor victories and minor losses. In January, the British captured Augusta, a future capital of Georgia. Soon after, they were forced to evacuate the city when Continental general Benjamin Lincoln sent in his troops. Throughout much of spring and summer, British and Continental troops chased each other across Georgia and South Carolina, until the terrible summer heat caused illness on both sides and forced the troops to a halt. In May, the British soldiers, under Sir Henry Clinton, launched attacks on Hudson River towns north of New York City. New York's governor, George Clinton, ordered the New York militia to fight back, but on June 1, the British captured the positions at Stony Point and Verplank's Point on the Hudson River. By the following month, however, colonial forces had recaptured these points.

Washington tried to organize the rebels' international allies in joint maneuvers against the British. In the fall of 1779, Washington wrote to Frenchman Comte d'Estaing,

General Benjamin Lincoln is dressed in the blue-and-gold Continental uniform in this portrait, painted by Charles Willson Peale between 1781 and 1783. Lincoln was the Continental commander in Charles Town, Virginia.

who was stationed with French warships off the coast of Georgia. He convinced Estaing to help attack British forces at Savannah, Georgia, but the assault failed, and Estaing sailed on to the West Indies. The conflict in Savannah shifted the focus of the war to the South. On December 26, 1779, General Clinton and five thousand British regulars sailed from New York City to prepare for an invasion of Charles Town, South Carolina, modern-day Charleston. George Washington saw this as an opportunity to recapture New York City, and he ordered several raids on the few British troops that were left behind to guard the city. Washington worried about the British army moving south, however, and he wrote to Congress about the "weak state of our force" there.

On April 8, 1780, General Clinton told Continental general Benjamin Lincoln to surrender Charles Town or Clinton would destroy the city. Lincoln refused, and five days later, the British began to bombard, or attack, the town with artillery. On May 8, after the patriots had spent nearly a month under siege, Clinton again demanded the surrender of the city. Lincoln again refused, and the British continued the attack. The city had largely been destroyed, and the citizens were exhausted. On May 9, Lieutenant Governor Christopher Gadsden, who earlier had refused to surrender, asked Lincoln to save the city from further destruction. Two petitions by citizens also asked Lincoln to give up. Finally, on May 12, he did. As the British and their Hessian mercenaries entered the city, Hessian captain Johann von Ewald said that the Colonial soldiers who had fought to defend Charles Town looked "extremely ragged, and on the whole the people looked greatly starved." Following this victory, General Clinton sailed back to New York and left British general Charles Cornwallis to capture other southern cities.

Washington saw the British strategy as an opportunity. He told Massachusetts governor James Bowdoin that the loss was "necessary to rouse" the colonials to fight harder. He also hoped that, by trying to capture cities so far apart from one another, the British would "dissipate their force . . . [giving us] opportunities of striking."

In January 1781, Continental soldiers in both Pennsylvania and New Jersey staged a mutiny to protest

British general Charles Cornwallis is portrayed here in a close-up of an 1817 painting by John Trumbull (the painting is shown in its entirety on page 69).

being unpaid, poorly equipped, and poorly fed. At Mount Kemble, New Jersey, the mutinous soldiers killed one officer and wounded another. Led by a group of sergeants and armed with cannons, these men began to march onward to the city of Philadelphia. They planned to take their protest to Congress and demand more money. Washington feared that many soldiers would join the British side to be properly paid for their service. Washington was a strong leader, and he firmly put down the mutinies. The leaders of the mutinies were executed, but Washington also put pressure on Congress to heed the soldiers' requests. He wrote to Congress that, because Congress had "punished guilt and supported authority, it becomes proper to do justice" and pay the soldiers who fought for their nation.

9. The World Turned Upside Down

Beginning in January 1781, Continental general Nathanael Greene led British general Charles Cornwallis on a chase through South Carolina and North Carolina. Greene met the larger British force in small skirmishes day after day. These tactics exhausted Cornwallis' men and made it difficult for the British to supply their scattered, isolated troops. The Continental army was proving itself a match for the British forces.

On March 1, 1781, Maryland ratified the Articles of Confederation. This document served as a temporary constitution, bridging the governmental gap between the Continental Congress of 1774 and the Constitution of the United States, written in 1787. The articles provided for strong, semi-independent state governments and for a centralized congress with limited federal powers. Maryland was the last state to adopt the articles as the law of the land. Five years after declaring its independence, America had a foundation for self-government.

Fighting continued in the South throughout 1781. Washington met with French commanders Comte de

To all to whom

The Articles of Confederation united the colonies as a nation of thirteen sovereign states. The articles described this federation as a "league of friendship." The document covers six sheets of parchment that are sewn together, and ends with the signatures of all thirteen delegates.

Rochambeau and Admiral Francois Joseph Paul, the comte de Grasse, on September 18, to plan a major offensive against General Cornwallis. By September 28, their combined forces were in place for a land and sea battle at Yorktown, Virginia.

On October 14, 1781, a French fleet of thirty-two warships and 3,200 troops under the command of Admiral Paul began bombing Cornwallis and his troops at Yorktown. On land Washington, Rochambeau, and the Marquis de Lafayette combined their forces to keep Cornwallis from escaping across the York River. After three days of bombing, Cornwallis offered the white

In John Trumbull's 1817 vision of the surrender at Yorktown, General Benjamin Lincoln, atop a white horse, accepts the surrender of Cornwallis, on foot, with French officers to the left and American officers, including Washington on horseback, to the right.

flag of surrender, and on October 19, the surrender was officially accepted by the triumphant Americans. The Continental army had decisively beaten the British army, the most powerful army on Earth. Legend has it that, as the British general signed the surrender orders, the disheartened British army band played an old Scottish tune, "The World Turned Upside Down."

Despite his satisfaction following the victory, General Washington was not completely happy. Soon after the incredible victory at Yorktown, Washington suffered a personal tragedy when his stepson, Jacky Custis, died of camp fever on November 5. Jacky had begun serving as an aide to his stepfather at Yorktown a few weeks before. Both of his beloved stepchildren had died at a young age.

In December 1782, Continental army officers, who had not been paid in years, petitioned Congress for their money and were rejected. The officers threatened to mutiny, but Washington intervened, gathering the angry officers for a meeting. With the officers crowded around him, Washington stared at Congress's letter of rejection for a moment. He then pulled out his glasses and said, "Gentlemen, you must pardon me. I have grown gray in your service and now find myself growing blind." Washington had suffered and sacrificed, as they had, and he asked them to be patient. The men were moved by his dedication, and the mutiny ended.

On December 4, 1783, Washington said good-bye to his officers and then headed to Annapolis, Maryland, where

Following the surrender of Lord Cornwallis, Washington ordered that all free blacks in the area of Yorktown were free to go, but that slaves who had fought for Britain were to be returned to their owners. Washington lived during a period of American history when slavery was largely accepted. When his father died, Washington inherited ten slaves, in addition to land. Over the years, Washington bought more land and more slaves. When Washington died in 1799, 316 slaves worked as planters, domestic servants, blacksmiths, coopers, carpenters, and shoemakers at his estate. Slaves at Mount Vernon worked from sunrise to sunset six days every week. Washington's attitude toward slavery changed as he grew older. As he led the Revolution, he began to realize that the struggle for independence and the enslavement of his fellow human beings were in opposition. In his private life, Washington followed his conscience. He made provisions in his will to arrange for the continued care and education of some of his former slaves. Publicly, however, Washington did not take a stand against slavery. As the delegates to the Constitutional Convention debated the foundations of democracy, Washington did not condemn the practice of enslavement. Washington worried that the southern states, whose economy relied heavily on slavery, would withdraw from the United States if slavery became a topic for debate. Seventy years later, his prediction was proven true, and the country was plunged into civil war.

On December 23, 1783, General Washington delivered his resignation to Congress, which was meeting in the Maryland State House in Annapolis. Washington was praised for withdrawing from the military. In doing so, he made certain that he could not seize control of the new nation as a military dictator. Instead he favored a civil government.

he handed Congress his resignation as commander in chief. He immediately set off for Mount Vernon and arrived home on Christmas Eve. His willing resignation of military power was remarkable. Many Americans thought he could have become the king of America or could have attempted to take over the government if he wished to do so. Washington had fought for the right of the people to govern themselves, however. By retiring his command, he embodied that belief.

10. Rebellion Against Law

After leading the colonies to independence, George Washington could hardly expect to return home and live as an average person. People came to Mount Vernon to meet the man in person, to ask for his advice, and to paint or sculpt his famous face. Some old friends visited the estate, including the Marquis de Lafayette, in August 1784. The Frenchman thought of Washington as a father figure. When he left after a stay of several weeks, the Marquis de Lafayette wrote, "I feel . . . love, respect and attachment for you."

Washington supported a strong federal government, but the Articles of Confederation, which had become law in 1781, passionately protected the powers of individual states. Congress could write treaties and laws, impose taxes, and declare war, but the Articles of Confederation did not give Congress the power to enforce any of these actions. Congress needed the states' permission to do this. For example, after the war, Congress asked the states to contribute money to pay Revolutionary war veterans. Many states did not want to give any money,

Washington's home at Mount Vernon, painted here in 1792, was richly furnished and often crowded with visitors. Washington was eager to resume the life of a Virginian planter and returned to public service only after he realized the new confederation of states was in danger.

and under the Articles of Confederation, Congress could not force them to do so. There was even talk of the states staging a rebellion against Congress and the Articles of Confederation.

Washington soon realized that the Articles of Confederation did not provide a strong foundation for the new nation. In 1783, he sent a letter to the leaders of every state. Washington argued that for America to be a true nation, all the states had to be united under one federal government, use only one currency, and be defended by a national military. Under the Articles of Confederation, the government could not run effectively.

Tensions came to a head in the summer of 1786, when a group of western Massachusetts farmers led by Daniel Shays attacked a courthouse. The farmers were furious over the increasingly high taxes they had been asked to pay. Washington was shocked and said that had someone told him "that this day, I should see such a formidable rebellion against the laws and constitutions of our own making . . . I should have thought him a bedlamite, a fit subject for a madhouse."

This 1787 relief cut from *Bickerstaff's Boston Almanack* is the only known image of Daniel Shays (*left*). Shays was an experienced Revolutionary war veteran who fought in the battles of Lexington, Bunker Hill, Ticonderoga, Stony Point, and Saratoga. After the war, America suffered from an economic depression. Many farmers lost their land and were thrown into debtors' prison after failing to pay their property taxes.

Washington was not surprised that civilians were angry at their government. After all, the imposition of unfair taxes had driven the colonists to revolution little more than ten years before. What concerned Washington was the fact that Shays and his followers rebelled violently against their legally elected representatives. In colonial America, the British Parliament had served as a distant, unfriendly governing body, but the new U.S. Congress was for and of the people.

To halt any further rebellion and to prevent the new nation from falling apart, the country's leaders called for a convention to rewrite the Articles of Confederation. In May 1787, fifty-five men met in Philadelphia at the Constitutional Convention. Washington made the trip from Mount Vernon in a horse-drawn carriage, and, just before his arrival in Philadelphia, a crowd of citizens gathered to get a glimpse of the famous man. Soldiers assembled around the carriage and saluted. As Washington entered downtown Philadelphia, according to his diary, " . . . the bells were chimed."

11. "Integrity and Firmness Is All I Can Promise"

Many famous men attended the convention. Benjamin Franklin, who was eighty-one years old, could not walk but still served as a delegate from Pennsylvania. Distinguished statesmen James Madison, Roger Sherman, and Gouverneur Morris all attended. However, no one was more respected and loved than the fifty-five-year-old George Washington, who was elected president of the proceedings. Washington saw that the central debates of the convention were about the relationship between the states and the federal government and the relationships among the states themselves. He thought that the only way for the states to survive was to unite under a strong, centralized government.

During the convention, the delegates debated how much power each state should have. Washington and many others supported Edmund Randolph's proposal, called the Virginia Plan. This proposal made the federal government stronger than the state governments. It also called for the determination of congressional representation by population, giving more populous states such as Virginia and New York more representatives in Congress. Smaller states opposed this plan and responded with the New Jersey Plan. Under this plan, the federal government remained small, and the state governments retained considerable power. The New Jersey Plan did, however, give Congress the power to tax the states directly. People who supported this plan, including William Paterson of New Jersey, wanted each state to have an equal number of representatives in Congress. A related debate raged over the status of slaves in determining the population, and, by extension, in determining the number of representatives each state would send to Congress.

After a great deal of discussion, the delegates compromised. Congress was formed as a bicameral legislature, meaning it contained two houses. The Senate was arranged along the New Jersey Plan, and every state, large or small, was allowed two representatives. The House of Representatives was structured along the guidelines of the Virginia Plan; the number of representatives from a state would be determined by that state's population. The Convention also decided on the 3/5 Compromise, which considered each slave as three-fifths of a person for the purposes of counting the population. When the Convention ended in mid-September, the Constitution was sent to the states for debate. Washington was eager to see the Constitution ratified, because he believed that self-government, never before seen in the modern world, was the foundation of the American Revolution. As president of the convention, Washington was the first man to sign the Constitution, and he returned home to Mount Vernon to rally support for the document. Nine states had to ratify the new constitution for it to become the law of the land. When New Hampshire became the final state to ratify the Constitution, on June 21, 1788, the document became law.

The Constitution provided for a modern, democratic system of government. It created an executive branch, headed by the president, a bicameral legislature, and an independent judicial branch. The Constitution set up a system of checks and balances to ensure that no single branch of the government could become too powerful. It did not include a declaration of rights for individuals, however.

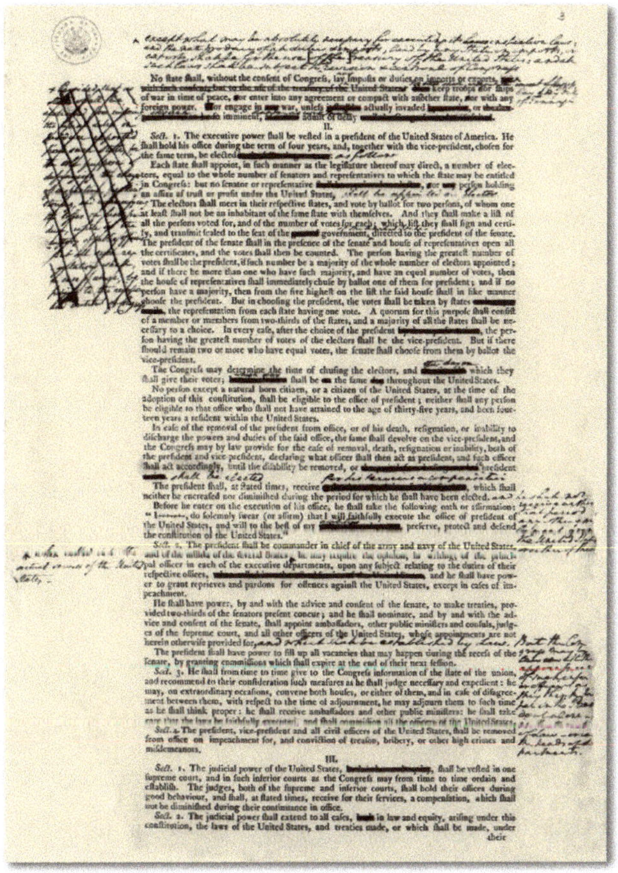

Washington's copy of the Constitution bears his notes on the new plan for democracy. Throughout his political career, he was a federalist, favoring a strong central government. At the convention, however, he refused to use his vast influence to determine the fate of the nation.

The loud cry for a bill of rights continued until finally, in 1791, the first ten amendments to the Constitution were adopted. Among other rights, they guarantee freedom of religion and freedom of speech for individuals and for the press.

People spoke of only one man as the future first president of the United States of America. Washington, long retired and getting older, was hesitant to take the job. He had made a promise when he had resigned as commander in chief in 1783 that he would never run for political office, and he did not want to go back on

Washington is shown arriving in Manhattan for his 1789 inauguration aboard a festive barge in Andrew Karoly and Louis Szanto's highly stylized 1953 painting.

his word. In early April 1789, the humble statesman wrote, in a letter to his friend Henry Knox, that he did not have the "political skill, abilities" or desire to serve, and that "integrity and firmness is all I can promise."

On April 6, the electoral votes were counted, and Washington was unanimously elected. John Adams was elected vice president. On April 14, 1789, the secretary of the Continental Congress, Charles Thomson of Philadelphia, arrived at Mount Vernon to deliver the official notice of Washington's election. Two days later, Washington set off for New York City, the seat of the new government. Along the way, he was greeted in every town by crowds, parades, and speeches. Arriving in New York on a barge specially decorated in red, white, and blue streamers, he was sworn in on the balcony of Wall Street's Federal Hall on April 30, 1789.

12. President of the United States

For more than a year after his inauguration, the new president of the United States lived in New York City. Then, in November 1790, the nation's capital moved to Philadelphia. In the beginning, the federal government was very small, and one of Washington's first tasks was to create departments within the government, each with a different responsibility, such as the departments of war, treasury, and state. During the first few years, Secretary of the Treasury Alexander Hamilton created a national bank to help stabilize the economy of the United States. In 1790, the states reached an agreement to pay soldiers the money due to them for their service during the war. The largest debts belonged to the northern states. The southern states agreed to assume some of the northern states' debt, and in return the northern states agreed that the future site of the federal capital could be in the

Opposite: Gilbert Stuart's 1800 oil portrait of George Washington portrays the president as a scholar, a statesman, and a leader of armies. The elegant setting is complete with columns and draped fabric.

Washington chose Pierre-Charles L'Enfant, a Frenchman who came to America at the age of twenty-two to fight in the Continental army, to design the nation's new capital. The city is organized to embody the grandeur of the principles of the U.S. Constitution. Broad avenues connect monuments, public squares, and green spaces like the spokes of a wheel.

South, on the Potomac River. This river divided Maryland and Virginia. These two states soon agreed to donate land to the federal government to create Washington, D.C.

At the president's temporary homes, first in New York City and then in Philadelphia, the Washingtons entertained guests and dignitaries from America and abroad in formal style. They thought it was important to show the power and strength of America in order to help the young nation become accepted as an equal by the governments of Europe. Martha Washington was known for her warm hospitality. Her friend Abigail Adams, the wife of Vice President John Adams, praised Martha as a per-

The Washingtons held weekly receptions, as illustrated in Daniel Huntington's painting. These parties were known as levees, after the traditional French ceremonies that accompanied the king waking in the morning. The Washingtons were not monarchs, but they used the vocabulary of European royalty to establish themselves as American aristocrats.

son for whom people naturally felt "Love and Esteem." Yet Martha Washington privately lamented that, although many women "would be extremely pleased" to be First Lady, she would "much rather be at home" at Mount Vernon.

As his four-year term as president came to an end, Washington decided that he did not want to serve again. He was tired, his body ached from arthritis, and he missed his home at Mount Vernon. Friends and statesmen urged him to reconsider. His old friend Representative James Madison of Virginia asked him to make "one more sacrifice . . . to the desire and interests of your country." Washington did not campaign for office, but when the electoral votes were counted in 1793, he was once again unanimously elected. Washington agreed to serve his country for a second term.

The first major crisis of Washington's presidency took place in 1794. In order to pay its debts, the federal government raised money through taxation. Products that were imported from overseas were already highly taxed. To collect additional money, Congress decided to levy an excise tax on whiskey. This tax primarily affected the farmers who lived on the frontier, as they were both the people who grew the grain to make the whiskey and the people who drank it. The excise tax was very unpopular, and few people paid it. Tax collectors tried to enforce the law, but their efforts were met with hostility. In July 1794, as many as seven hundred local militiamen surrounded

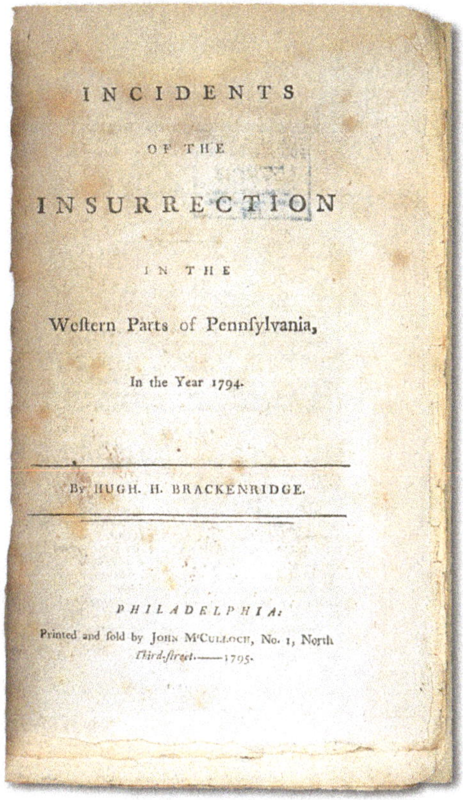
INCIDENTS
OF THE
INSURRECTION
IN THE
Western Parts of Pennsylvania,
In the Year 1794.
By HUGH. H. BRACKENRIDGE.
PHILADELPHIA:
Printed and sold by JOHN M'CULLOCH, No. 1, North Third-street.——1795.

Among the titles in Washington's personal library was Hugh Henry Brackenridge's 1795 account of the Pennsylvanian Whiskey Rebellion.

the house of a regional tax collector in western Pennsylvania. They shot at the house and eventually burned it down. On August 1, seven thousand rebels, including the state militia, gathered outside Pittsburgh—in the very field where Washington had fought with Braddock against the French almost forty years before—and threatened to secede from the United States in protest of the tax.

Government leaders were not sure how to react. The new secretary of state, Edmund Randolph, suggested sending a commission to investigate the situation. Alexander Hamilton wanted to send troops to put down the revolt. President Washington stayed calm. He sent three commissioners to study the situation and later ordered that a force of nearly thirteen thousand soldiers be mustered. As Attorney General William Bradford wrote, Washington demonstrated both the moderation and the firmness of a representative government.

While the army was preparing to march, what had become known as the Whiskey Rebellion died down. The rebels did not want to fight Washington's Western Army. The leaders of the rebels voted to pay the tax, but a few hundred people remained outside of Pittsburgh ready to fight. In the last week of September, when Washington ordered the troops to march toward the remaining rebels, the rebels lost their will to fight. Washington's patience and show of strength had defeated the rebels.

In August 1794, the militias of four states were organized to suppress the west Pennsylvanian rebels. In a painting attributed to Frederick Kemmelmeyer, Washington, on a white horse, inspects the Western Army at Maryland's Fort Cumberland.

Washington had made a powerful statement about the new government to audiences both at home and abroad. To Americans, Washington's actions were a clear message that they were free to disagree with and peacefully demonstrate against the laws made by their representatives. However, they could not disobey the law or resort to violence. Washington wanted to show the people that theirs was a legitimate government making legitimate laws. Washington also wanted to demonstrate to Spain and Britain, both countries with colonial claims bordering America, that the new nation was well run. The president knew that he needed to be strong with foreign powers so close to home.

John Trumbull painted Chief Justice John Jay around 1794. In America, Republicans hoped for a war with Great Britain, while Federalists shouted for war with France. Washington wanted peace, and Jay was sent to Britain to carry out the president's mission.

As the Whiskey Rebellion was ending, the chief justice of the Supreme Court, John Jay, was in London meeting with the king of Britain. Jay sought to improve relations between Britain and its former American colonies. America's economy was largely dependent on trade with Britain. Britain and France were at war with each other, and the British were stopping American ships on the Atlantic Ocean and accusing them of trading with the French. While Jay sought an immediate solution to America's economic problems, the country debated whether to take sides or remain neutral in this protracted European conflict.

According to the terms of Jay's Treaty, the British agreed to leave their forts on the American frontier and to pay for American cargo seized on the high seas by British ships. In addition, the British agreed to let American ships trade with the West Indies, though they limited the size and destination of shipments.

Many Americans were unhappy with Jay's Treaty, especially with the limits it placed on America's right to trade. Britain also benefited from trade with the United States, so why should America be forced to compromise? The Senate and the House of Representatives fiercely debated the treaty. The Constitution gave the power to approve treaties to the Senate and the power over government funds to the House. Both houses would have to agree on the terms of the treaty if it were to be passed. Washington was patient during this debate. He refused to sign or to veto the treaty for several months. He was not completely satisfied with the treaty himself, but he realized that it was the best that could be done at the time. Eventually, the controversy subsided. People who had disliked the treaty at first later decided that it would help the economy to grow.

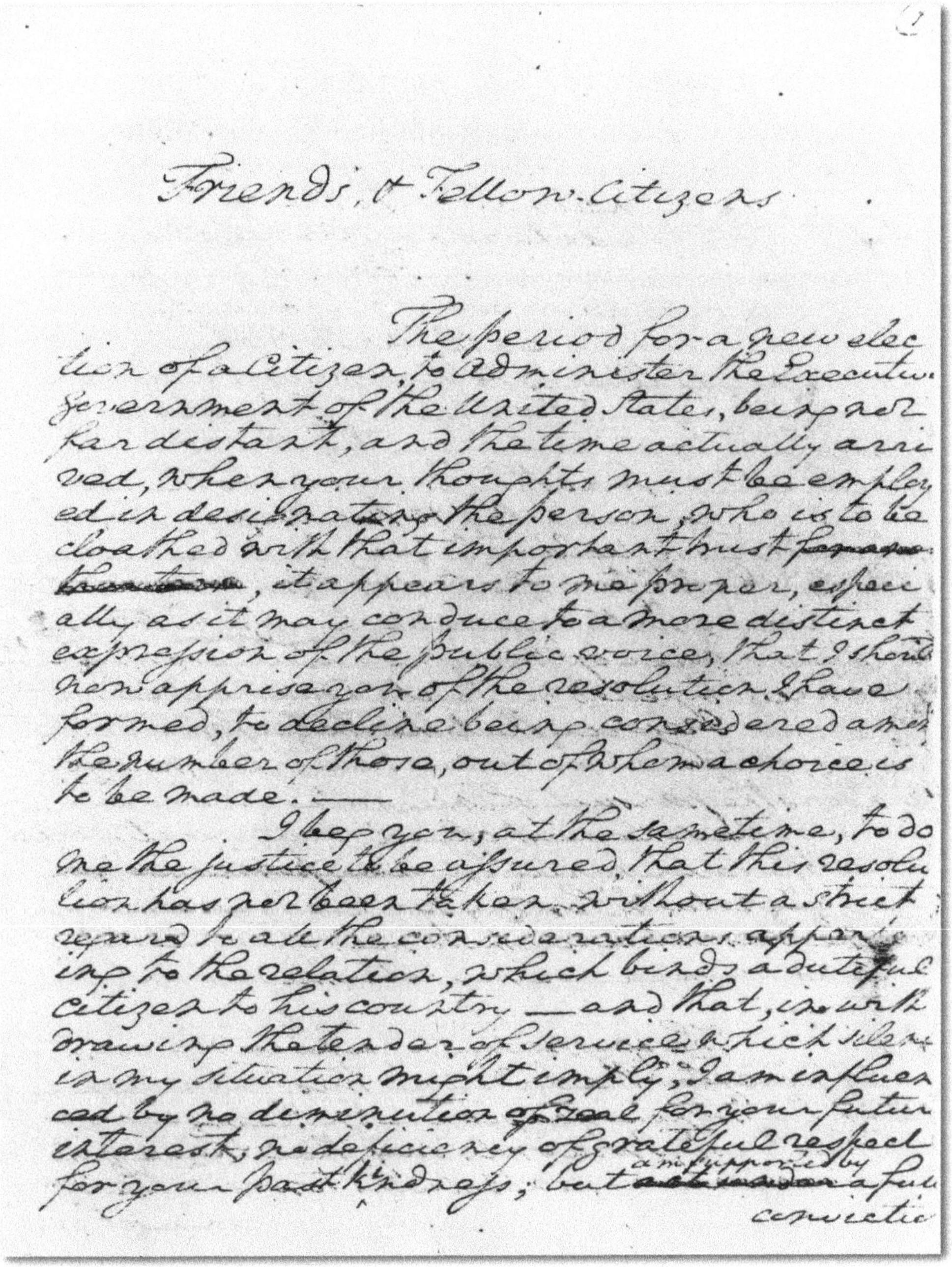

Friends, & Fellow-Citizens.

The period for a new election of a Citizen, to administer the Executive Government of the United States, being not far distant, and the time actually arrived, when your thoughts must be employed in designating the person, who is to be cloathed with that important trust, it appears to me proper, especially as it may conduce to a more distinct expression of the public voice, that I should now apprise you of the resolution I have formed, to decline being considered among the number of those, out of whom a choice is to be made.—

I beg you, at the same time, to do me the justice to be assured, that this resolution has not been taken, without a strict regard to all the considerations appertaining to the relation, which binds a dutiful citizen to his country — and that, in withdrawing the tender of service which silence in my situation might imply, I am influenced by no diminution of zeal for your future interest, no deficiency of grateful respect for your past kindness; but am supported by a full conviction

Washington's farewell address was the product of a unique collaboration between Washington, James Madison, and Alexander Hamilton. In it, Washington considers his triumphs and defeats, and he asks his fellow citizens to make sure "that the free Constitution, which is the work of your hands, may be sacredly maintained."

To the president, the issue at stake in the debate over Jay's Treaty resembled that of the Whiskey Rebellion. A self-governing majority had decided a political issue in a legitimate way, and a minority should not be able to exercise its will illegally simply because it disagreed. Decisions could only be reversed through the same Constitutional process by which they had been made. This process is what ensures a legitimate government elected by the people.

Washington almost certainly could have been re-elected for a third term, but the sixty-four-year-old president was worn out and ready to go home to Mount Vernon. On September 19, 1796, five months before his term ended, he published his farewell address in the *American Daily Advertiser*, a Philadelphia newspaper. It appeared under a small headline, "To the PEOPLE of the United States/Friends and fellow citizens." Washington wrote about self-interest and the need for the young nation to keep its independence. He urged the country not to become permanently allied with another nation and to always control its own "duty and interest."

Washington had freely given up his power once again. Two-term vice president John Adams was elected as the second president and was inaugurated on March 4, 1797. Washington watched the ceremony and then returned to his home at Mount Vernon with his wife.

13. "A Wise, a Good, and a Great Man"

Washington hoped to return home and live out his days in peace and privacy, but alas, he was the most famous man in North America. Many people wanted to meet the great general and statesman. Mount Vernon was regularly flooded with guests and workmen, coming to do repairs on the long-ignored estate. When he had been home less than three weeks, he wrote to a friend in Philadelphia, "I am already surrounded by Joiners, Masons, Painters, &ca. And such is my anxiety to get out of their hands, that I scarcely have a room to put a friend into or to set in myself, without the Music of hammers, or the odoriferous smell of Paint." Even strangers came by to see the great man. Washington was polite, and the manners of the eighteenth century required that he greet everyone respectfully. Despite these interruptions, Washington was happy to be at home. He awoke early every morning, and after breakfast at seven o'clock, "I mount my horse and ride around my farms." He was the master of Mount Vernon and made sure that it ran as well as possible.

Nathaniel Currier's lithograph of Washington in the fields of Mount Vernon shows the retired president in the costume of a gentleman farmer. Washington described his career as a farmer as "the most pleasing occupation of [his] life."

In the summer of 1798, America faced a new war, this time with France. After Jay's Treaty was signed with Britain, France began raiding American ships on the Atlantic Ocean. During negotiations, three French agents, known as X, Y, and Z, suggested that the American delegates bribe the French government, requesting more than $10 million in gifts and loans. Word of this scandal, which became known as the XYZ Affair, reached America, and the people were outraged at the insult. They prepared for war with France.

President John Adams approached George Washington and asked that he command the army in case of an invasion. Washington was very eager for this new post and accepted it with great energy. He did not give up on diplomacy, however, and Washington urged Adams to try negotiating again. President Adams did, and war was avoided.

The public was shocked and saddened by Washington's death. This unattributed print is one of several that depict the former president on his deathbed. Two eyewitness accounts were also published in the following years.

Washington insisted on riding his horse to survey his Mount Vernon lands every morning, even when the weather was terrible. In early December 1799, he caught a throat infection while riding in harsh winter weather. The infection weakened him, and on December 14, 1799, he died in his bed. George Washington was sixty-seven years old.

Martha Washington was too upset to attend her husband's funeral. She closed up their bedroom and moved herself to a tiny room on the third floor of Mount Vernon.

A new granddaughter, Frances Parke Lewis, born only twenty days before Washington died, was Martha's only consolation.

In his will, Washington made arrangements to free all of his slaves after the death of his wife. Martha chose to free all of these slaves before her death, on January 1, 1801. More than half of the slaves at Mount Vernon, however, belonged to the estate of Martha's first husband and could not be freed by the Washingtons. Martha died at Mount Vernon on May 22, 1802, and

On December 26, 1799, a crowd of mourners, bearing an empty box meant to represent Washington's coffin, processed through Philadelphia's High Street. The scene is depicted in an 1800 engraving by William R. Birch. Similar memorial services were held across America, attesting to Washington's mythic status.

A mourning locket bears a miniature painting of a woman grieving over the death of Washington on the front *(left)* and a plait of George and Martha's intertwined hair on the back *(right)*. During the eighteenth and nineteenth centuries, jewelry designed to mark the death of a loved one was common. The deceased's hair was used in broaches, rings, and lockets.

was buried in the family tomb with her husband and daughter.

• • • • •

More than two hundred years after it was written, Washington's farewell address of 1796 remains one of the most famous documents in American history. Even more important than Washington's words were his actions. As the first president of a country in the history

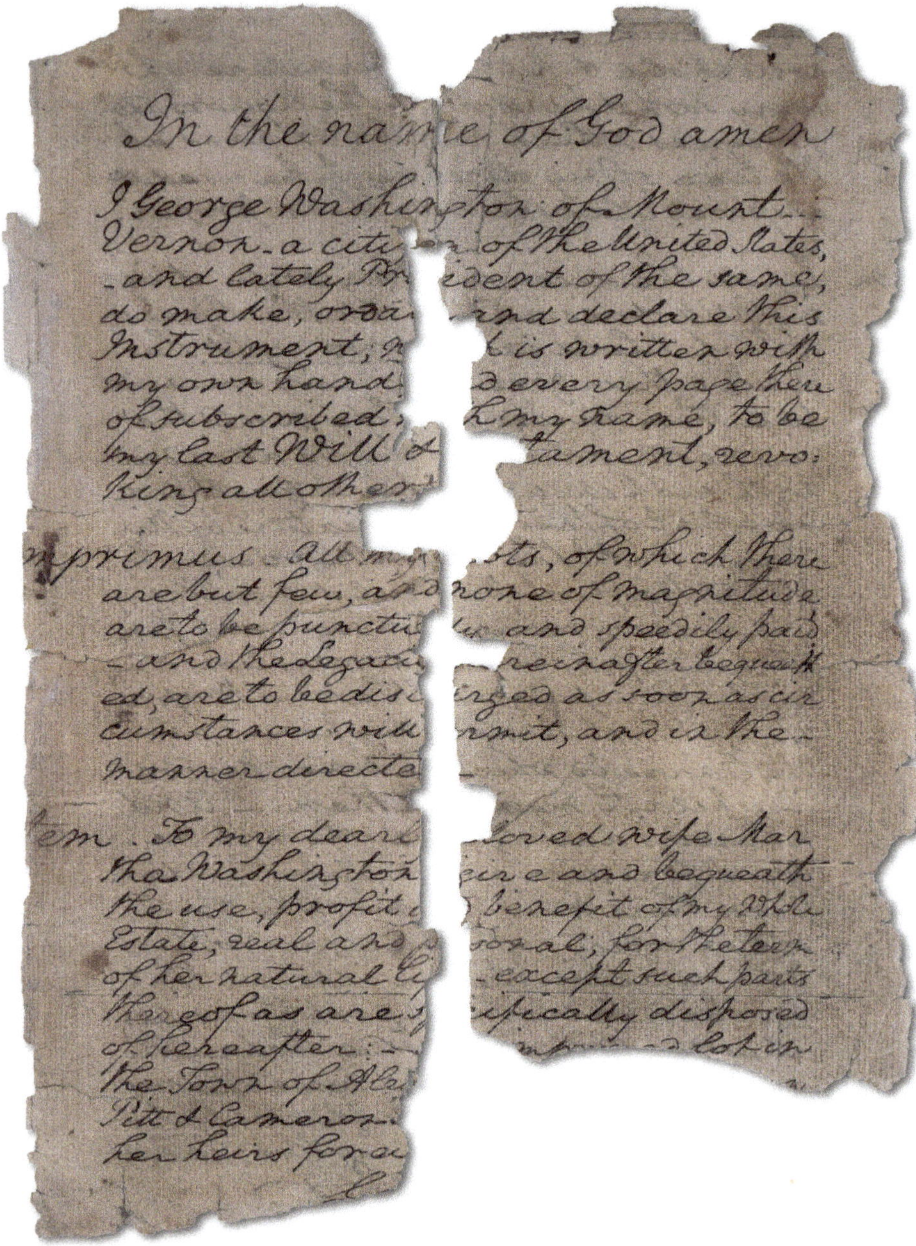

In the name of God amen

I George Washington of Mount
Vernon a citi of the United States,
and lately Pr ident of the same,
do make, ordai and declare this
Instrument, w is written with
my own hand d every page there
of subscribed, h my name, to be
my last Will & tament, revo:
king all other

Imprimus. All m ts, of which there
are but few, a none of magnitude
are to be punctu ly and speedily paid
and the Legacie hereafter bequeath
ed, are to be dis rged as soon as cir
cumstances will mit, and in the
manner directe

Item. To my dearl loved wife Mar
tha Washington ive and bequeath
the use, profit benefit of my whole
Estate, real and sonal, for the term
of her natural li except such parts
thereof as are s ecifically disposed
of hereafter: lot in
the Town of Ale
Pitt & Cameron
her heirs for e

George Washington's twenty-nine-page will is still kept in the archives of the Fairfax County Circuit Court. In the months after Washington's death, his will was printed as a pamphlet and distributed across the country to admirers of the former president who were eager to read his final written words.

of the world, Washington had no example to follow. He could have stayed in power and perhaps become a life-long ruler. Had Washington remained in office indefinitely, what would have happened to the idea of an elected government "of the people, for the people and by the people"? Throughout history, people have battled for power. Few people have given it up willingly. Even Britain's king George III understood the importance of Washington's resignation. He called Washington "the greatest character of the age."

Fourteen years after Washington's death, Thomas Jefferson wrote of the country's first president:

> *Perhaps the strongest feature in his character was prudence, never acting until every circumstance, every consideration, was maturely weighed . . . once decided, [he went] through with his purpose, whatever obstacles opposed. His integrity was most pure, his justice the most inflexible I have ever known. . . . He was indeed, in every sense of the words, a wise, a good, and a great man.*

Timeline

1732 George Washington is born on February 22.

1748 Washington begins his career as a surveyor.

1752 Lawrence Washington dies, and Mount Vernon is passed to George Washington.

1754 From April to May, Washington leads the Virginia militia against the French at Fort Duquesne.

1755 On July 9, Washington is defeated by the French at Monongahela River but is recognized for his bravery.

1758 Washington's troops capture Fort Duquesne in November.

Washington is elected to a term in Virginia's House of Burgesses.

1759 On January 6, Washington marries Martha Dandridge Custis.

1774 Washington attends the First Continental Congress in Philadelphia.

1775 The Battle of Lexington and Concord takes place on April 19.

The Second Continental Congress begins on May 10. Washington attends and is voted commander in chief on June 15.

1776 On July 4, the Declaration of Independence is adopted.

On December 25, Washington crosses the Delaware River to launch a surprise attack on the British troops at Trenton.

1777 On October 17, General Horatio Gates defeats British general John Burgoyne at Saratoga, New York.

In December, Washington settles in with his troops at Valley Forge, Pennsylvania, for the winter.

1778 Baron von Steuben arrives at Valley Forge to train the army.

1781 On March 1, the Articles of Confederation are adopted.

On October 14, the Americans and the French begin bombarding Yorktown, Virginia.

On October 19, British general Lord Cornwallis's surrender is officially accepted.

1783 In December, Washington reads his farewell orders to the Continental army and resigns as commander in chief.

1787 Washington presides at the Constitutional Convention in Philadelphia from May to September.

1789 On April 30, Washington is inaugurated as president of the United States.

1793 Washington is unanimously reelected as president.

1796 On September 19, Washington publishes his farewell address.

1797 On March 4, Washington retires as president of the United States.

1798 Following the XYZ Affair with France, Washington is appointed commander of the American army.

1799 After catching a throat infection, Washington dies on December 14.

1802 On May 22, Martha Washington dies.

Glossary

adjutant (AY-juh-tunt) A staff officer of the army who works closely with the commanding officer.

amendments (uh-MEND-ments) Additions or changes to the Constitution.

bicameral legislature (by-KAM-rul LEH-jis-lay-chur) A law-making body consisting of two parts, such as the Senate and the House of Representatives in the U.S. Congress.

camp fever (KAMP FEE-vur) An infectious disease carried by insects that live on the bodies of people and animals.

commandeer (kah-mun-DEER) To seize for military purposes.

commander in chief (kuh-MAN-dur IN CHEEF) The person in charge of all armed forces.

currency (KUR-en-see) The money in use in a country.

demoted (dih-MOHT-ed) To have lowered the rank of an officer.

dissolved (dih-ZOLVD) To have broken down.

dysentery (DIH-sun-ter-ee) A disease marked by severe diarrhea and the passage of mucus and blood.

evacuated (ee-VA-kyoo-ayt-ed) To have left an area immediately because it is not safe.

excise tax (EK-syz TAKS) A tax that the government puts on goods that are produced in its own country.

fortification (for-tih-fih-KAY-shun) A strong building or place that can be defended against an enemy.

garrison (GAR-ih-sun) A group of soldiers stationed at a fort.

House of Burgesses (HOWS UV BUR-jes-ez) The elected legislature of the Virginia Colony.

immunity (ih-MYOO-nuh-tee) The ability to resist infection by a particular disease.

legitimate (lih-JIH-tuh-mut) Something acceptable according to the law.

mercenary (MER-suh-ner-ee) Referring to any professional soldier serving in a foreign army for pay.

militia (muh-LIH-shuh) A group of volunteer or citizen soldiers who are organized to assemble in emergencies.

mortars (MOR-turz) Short-barreled cannons used to send explosives high into the air.

mutiny (MYOO-tin-ee) A revolt of a ship's crew or of soldiers against their commanding officer or officers.

plantation (plan-TAY-shun) A very large farm where crops such as tobacco or cotton were grown.

proposal (pruh-POH-zul) A suggestion, or a plan.

ratify (RA-tih-fy) To approve or agree to something in a formal way.

reinforcements (ree-in-FORS-ments) Anything that strengthens, specifically additional troops or warships to make stronger those already sent.

resign (rih-ZYN) To step down from a position.

scurvy (SKUR-vee) A disease resulting from a deficiency of vitamin C, characterized by weakness and bleeding from mucus membranes.

secede (sih-SEED) To withdraw from a group or a country.

skirmishes (SKUR-mish-ez) Brief fights or encounters.

smallpox (SMOL-poks) A serious and often fatal disease that causes a rash and leaves deep scars on the skin.

sovereignty (SAH-ver-en-tee) Supreme rule or power.

stockade (stah-KAYD) A line of stout posts set firmly to form a defense, operating as a large fence.

survey (ser-VAY) To measure land.

tactics (TAK-tiks) Plans to win a battle.

treaty (TREE-tee) An official agreement, signed and agreed upon by each party.

tuberculosis (too-ber-kyuh-LOH-sis) A serious infectious disease that affects the lungs.

unanimous (yoo-NA-nih-mus) Having the agreement of all.

veto (VEE-toh) Not to authorize laws proposed by another department or branch of government.

Additional Resources

For more information about George Washington, check out the following books and Web sites:

Books

Davis, Burke. *George Washington and the American Revolution*. New York: Random House, 1975.

Korman, Justine, Ron Fontes, and Justine Fontes. *George Washington: Soldier, Hero, President*. New York: DK Publishing, 2001.

Marrin, Albert and Donna L. Brooks. *George Washington and the Founding of a Nation*. New York: Dutton Books, 2001.

Web Sites

Due to the changing nature of Internet links, PowerPlus Books has developed an online list of Web sites related to the subject of this book. This site is updated regularly. Please use this link to access the list:

www.powerkidslinks.com/lalt/washington/

Bibliography

Brookhiser, Richard. *Founding Father: Rediscovering George Washington*. New York: Free Press, 1997.

Cunliffe, Marcus. *George Washington: Man and Monument*. New York: Little, Brown & Company, 1958.

Eaton, Jeanette. *Leader by Destiny: George Washington, Man and Patriot*. New York: Harcourt Brace, 1938.

Flexner, James Thomas. *Washington: The Indispensable Man*. London: Collins, 1969.

Foster, Genevieve. *George Washington's World*. New York: Charles Scribner's Sons, 1941.

Rasmussen, William M. S. and Robert S. Tilton. *George Washington: The Man Behind the Myths*. Charlottesville, Virginia: University Press of Virginia, 1999.

Index

A
Adams, Abigail, 85
Adams, John, 47, 81, 92, 95
Adams, Samuel, 35, 39, 47
Articles of Confederation, 67, 73–76
Attucks, Crispus, 35

B
Battle of Brooklyn, 49
Battle of Bunker Hill, 40
Battle of Harlem Heights, 49
Battle of Kip's Bay, 49
Battle of Monmouth, 62
Battle of the Brandywine, 51
Battle of the Monongahela River, 28
Battle of White Plains, 49
Boston Massacre, 35
Boston Tea Party, 35
Bowdoin, James, 65
Braddock, General Edward, 27–28
Bradford, William, 87
Burgoyne, John, 55

C
Clinton, Henry, 63–65
Coercive Acts, 35. *See also* Intolerable Acts.
Congress, 5, 51, 57, 61, 66, 70, 72, 74, 78, 86
Constitution, 79
Constitutional Convention, 76, 78
Continental army, 5
Continental Congress, 47, 67
Conway, Thomas, 56
Cornwallis, Charles (British general), 65, 67, 69
Custis, Jacky (stepson), 31, 70
Custis, Martha Dandridge, 31. *See also* Washington, Martha.
Custis, Patsy (stepdaughter), 31, 33

D
Dawes, William, 39
Deane, Silas, 55
Declaration of Independence, 47–48
Dinwiddie, Governor Robert, 19–20, 22–24, 27, 29

F
Fairfax, Anne, 9–10. See also Washington, Anne.
Fairfax, George William, 13
Fairfax, William, 10
Fairfax County Resolves, 36–37
Ferry Farm, 8, 10
First Continental Congress, 37
Fort Duquesne, 25, 29, 31
Fort Le Boeuf, 20, 22–23
Fort Necessity, 25, 27
Fort Pitt, 31
Fort Washington, 45
Franklin, Benjamin, 47, 55, 77
French and Indian War, the, 25–29, 31, 33
Fry, Colonel Joshua, 24

G
Gadsden, Lieutenant Governor Christopher, 65
Gage, Thomas, 38
Gates, Horatio, 55–56
Genn, James (surveyor), 13
George III, king of Great Britain, 34, 40, 43, 99
Great Meadows, 25
Greene, Nathanael (patriot general), 67

H

Half King, 23
Hamilton, Alexander, 82, 87
Hancock, John, 39, 47
Henry, Patrick, 57
Hessians, 45, 50
Howe, Richard (British vice admiral), 48
Howe, William (British general), 41, 43–44, 47, 51, 54, 62

I

Intolerable Acts, 35–36, 40. *See also* Coercive Acts.

J

Jay, John, 89–90
Jay's Treaty, 90, 92, 94
Jefferson, Thomas, 36, 47, 55, 99

L

Lafayette, Marquis de, 69, 73
land speculating, 16
Lee, Henry, 5
Lee, Thomas, 16
Lewis, Frances Parke (granddaughter), 96
Lincoln, Benjamin, 63, 65
Livingston, Robert, 47

M

Madison, James, 77
Mifflin, Thomas, 56
Morris, Gouverneur, 77
Mount Vernon, 9–13, 18–19, 33–34, 72–73, 76, 79, 86, 92–93, 95–96
Murray, John, earl of Dunmore, 36

P

Parliament, 34
Pitcairn, John (British major), 39
Prescott, Samuel, 39

S

Second Continental Congress, 40
Shays, Daniel, 75–76
Sherman, Roger, 47, 77
smallpox, 18, 29
Smith, Francis, 39
Steuben, Baron Friedrich von, 61–62
Sullivan, John (patriot general), 48

V

Valley Forge, Pennsylvania, 57, 61
Vernon, Edward (British admiral), 9
Virginia Plan, 77–78

W

Wakefield Farm, 6
Washington, Anne, 18
Washington, Augustine (father), 5
Washington, Augustine (half brother), 7, 10
Washington, Charles (brother), 7
Washington, Elizabeth (sister), 7
Washington, John Augustine (brother), 7
Washington, Lawrence (half brother), 7, 9–13, 16, 18–19
Washington, Martha (wife), 42–43, 57, 85–86, 95–97. *See also* Custis, Martha Dandridge.
Washington, Mary Ball (mother), 6
Washington, Mildred (sister), 7
Washington, Samuel (brother), 7
Washington, Sarah (niece), 18
Whiskey Rebellion, 86–89, 92

About the Author

Daniel C. Gedacht graduated with an undergraduate degree in American history from Clark University in 1993. He received a master's degree in International Affairs from American University in Washington, D.C., and a master's degree in economics from Korea University, in Seoul, Korea, in 1997. He became interested in American history as a child when he learned that he has the same birthday as Abraham Lincoln. After several years of living in South Korea, he currently lives in Italy, where he is writing a book of travel fiction.

Primary Sources

Cover: *The Signing of the Constitution*. Howard Chandler Christy, oil on canvas. **Page 4:** *George Washington.* Gilbert Stuart, oil on canvas, circa 1785. **Page 6:** Bible record. Mount Vernon Ladies' Association. **Page 7:** *The Birth-Place of Washington*. Currier & Ives, lithograph, circa 1860, Mount Vernon Ladies' Association. **Page 9:** *Lawrence Washington*. John Wollaston, oil on canvas, 1738. **Page 10:** *A Plan of Major Law. Washington's Turnip Field as Survey'd by me*. George Washington, February 27, 1747, Manuscript Division of the Library of Congress. **Page 12:** Survey notebook. October 1, 1747, George Washington Papers in the Manuscript Division of the Library of Congress. **Page 15:** George Washington's field compass. Alexandria-Washington Lodge. **Page 17:** George Washington's map of Ohio, 1753, Geography and Map Division of the Library of Congress. **Page 19:** Robert Dinwiddie. Artist unknown, oil paint, circa 1750, Colonial Williamsburg Foundation. **Page 20:** Lead plate, 1749, Virginia Historical Society. **Page 21:** *A Map of the Country on the Ohio & Muskingum Rivers.* Thomas Jefferys, 1768, Geography and Map Division of the Library of Congress. **Page 24:** Washington and Gist crossing the Allegheny River. Attributed to Daniel Huntington, oil on canvas, mid-19th century, Mount Vernon Ladies' Association. **Page 26:** *Plan of Fort Le Quesne*. Thomas Jefferys, engraving, 1768, Geography and Map Division of the Library of Congress. **Page 28:** *Washington as a Captain in the French and Indian War*. Junius Brutus Stearns, oil on canvas, circa 1851, Virginia Museum of Fine Arts. **Page 30:** *Washington as Colonel of the Virginia Regiment*. Charles Willson Peale, oil on canvas, 1772, Washington and Lee University. **Page 33:** *Martha Dandrigde Custis*. John Wollaston, oil on canvas, 1757, Washington and Lee University. **Page 35:** *King George III*. Attributed to the studio of Allan Ramsay, oil on canvas, circa 1761-1762, Colonial Williamsburg Foundation. **Page 37:** Raleigh Tavern. Held by the Colonial Williamsburg Foundation. **Page 38:** *A View of the Town of Concord*. Sidney L. Smith, engraving, 1775, New York Public Library. **Page 41:** *View of the Attack on Bunker's Hill, With the Burning of Charles Town, June 17, 1775*. Lodge, engraving, U.S. Naval Historical Center. **Page 42:** Recruitment broadside. Reproduction of engraving by B. Jones, circa 1775, Broadside Collection of the Prints and Photographs Division of the Library of Congress. **Page 44:** *A plan of the town of Boston and its environs, with the lines, batteries, and incampments of the British and American armies.* Sir Thomas Hyde Page, pen-and-ink and watercolor on paper, 1776, Map Division of the

Library of Congress. **Page 46:** *A Plan of New York Island, with part of Long Island, Staten Island & East New Jersey* . William Faden, engraving, 1777, Geography and Map Division of the Library of Congress. **Page 48:** *Admiral Richard Howe*. J. Chapman, Anne S. K. Brown Military Collection. **Page 52–53:** *George Washington Crossing the Delaware*. Emmanuel Gottlieb Leutze, oil on canvas, 1851, Metropolitan Museum of Art. **Page 55:** *Horatio Gates*. Charles Willson Peale, oil on canvas, 1782, Independence National Historic Park. **Page 56:** *The Surrender of General Burgoyne*. John Trumbull, oil on canvas, 1817, Architect of the Capitol. **Page 58–59**: *The March to Valley Forge*. William T. Trego, 1883, Valley Forge Historic National Park. **Page 60:** *Frederick William Augustus, Baron von Steuben*. Charles Willson Peale, oil on canvas, circa 1782–1784, Independence National Historic Park. **Page 61:** *Carte de l'affaire de Montmouth*. Michel du Chesnoy, pen-and-ink and watercolor on paper, 1778, Geography and Map Division of the Library of Congress. **Page 64:** *General Benjamin Lincoln*. Charles Willson Peale, oil on canvas, circa 1781–1783, Independence National Historical Park. **Page 68:** The Articles of Confederation. National Archives and Records Adminstration. **Page 69:** *The Surrender of Lord Cornwallis*. John Trumbull, oil on canvas, 1817, Architect of the Capitol. **Page 72:** *General George Washington Resigning His Commission*. John Trumbull, oil on canvas, 1817, Architect of the Capitol. **Page 74:** *A View of Mount Vernon*. Artist unknown, oil on canvas, circa 1792, National Gallery of Art. **Page 75:** *Daniel Shays and Job Shattuck*. Artist unknown, 1787, National Portrait Gallery. **Page 79:** Draft of the U.S. Constitution. George Washington Papers in the Manuscript Division of the Library of Congress. **Page 80:** *Washington Arrives in Manhattan for Inauguration, 1789*. Andrew Karoly and Louis Szanto, 1953. **Page 83:** *George Washington*. Gilbert Stuart, oil on canvas, circa 1800, New York Public Library. **Page 84:** Plan of Washington. J. Good, engraving, 1793, Geography and Map Division of the Library of Congress. **Page 85:** Reception given by Martha Washington. Daniel Huntington. **Page 87:** *Incidents of the insurrection in the western parts of Pennsylvania, in the year 1794*. Hugh Henry Brackenridge, 1795, New York Public Library. **Page 88:** *Washington Reviewing the Western Army at Fort Cumberland, Maryland*. Attributed to Frederick Kemmelmeyer, oil on canvas, Metropolitan Museum of Art. **Page 89:** *John Jay*. John Trumbull, oil on canvas, circa 1794, John Jay Homestead State Historic Site. **Page 91:** Washington's Farewell Address. New York Public Library. **Page 94:** *Washington at Mount Vernon*. Currier & Ives, lithograph. **Page 95:** *G. WASHINGTON in his last Illness attended by Doc rs Craik and Brown*. Hand-toned print, circa 1800, Mount Vernon Ladies' Association. **Page 96:** *High Street from the Country Market-place, Philadelphia* . William R. Birch, engraving, circa 1800, Independence National Historical Park. **Page 97:** Memorial locket, 18th century. **Page 98:** *Last Will and Testament of George Washington*. Fairfax County Circuit Court.

Credits

Photo Credits

Cover (portrait), pp. 30, 33 Washington-Custis-Lee Collection, Washington and Lee University, Lexington, Va.; cover (background) Art Resource, NY; p. 4 © Francis G. Mayer/CORBIS; pp. 6, 7, 9, 24, 95 courtesy of the Mt. Vernon Ladies' Association; pp. 12, 14, 79 Library of Congress, Manuscript Division; p. 15 photo by Arthur W. Pierson, courtesy of the Alexandria-Washington Lodge, No. 22, A.F. & A.M.; pp. 17, 21, 26, 44, 46, 61, 84 Library of Congress Geography and Map Division; pp. 19, 35, 37 Colonial Williamsburg Foundation; p. 20 courtesy of the Virginia Historical Society, Richmond, Virginia; p. 28 Virginia Museum of Fine Arts, Richmond, Gift of Edgar William and Bernice Chrysler Garbisch; p. 38 the Phelps Stokes Collection, Miriam and Ira D. Wallach Division of Art, Prints, and Photographs, the New York Public Library, Astor, Lenox, and Tilden Foundations; p. 41 courtesy U.S. Naval Historical Center; p. 42 Prints and Photographs Division Library of Congress; p. 48 Anne S. K. Brown Military Collection, Brown University Library; pp. 52–53 © Bettmann/CORBIS; pp. 55, 60, 64, 96 Independence National Historical Park; pp. 56, 66, 69, 72 Architect of the Capitol; pp. 58–59 National Center for the American Revolution/ The Valley Forge Historical Society; p. 68 Old Military and Civil Records, National Archives and Records Administration; p. 74 National Gallery of Art, Washington, gift of Edgar William and Bernice Chrysler Garbisch; p. 75 National Portrait Gallery, Smithsonian Institution/Art Resource, NY; pp. 80, 85, 94 © SuperStock; p. 83 Collections of the New York Public Library, Astor, Lenox, and Tilden Foundations; p. 87 Rare Books & Manuscripts Collection, New York Public Library Astor, Lenox, and Tilden Foundations; p. 88 the Metropolitan Museum of Art, gift of Edgar William and Bernice Chrysler Garbisch, 1963; p. 89 courtesy of the John Jay Homestead State Historic Site, New York State Office of Parks, Recreation and Historic Preservation; p. 91 George Washington Papers, Manuscripts and Archives Division, the New York Public Library, Astor, Lenox, and Tilden Foundations; p. 97 Special Collections of the University of Virginia Library; p. 98 photograph by Mark Gulezian, courtesy of the Mount Vernon Ladies' Association.

Editor Gillian Houghton

Series Design Laura Murawski

Layout Design Corinne L. Jacob

Photo Researcher Jeffrey Wendt